William Shakespeare's
Henry V
In Plain and Simple English

BookCaps Study Guides

www.SwipeSpeare.com

Table of Contents

About This Series

The "Classic Retold" series started as a way of telling classics for the modern reader—being careful to preserve the themes and integrity of the original. Whether you want to understand Shakespeare a little more or are trying to get a better grasps of the Greek classics, there is a book waiting for you!

The series is expanding every month. Visit BookCaps.com to see all the books in the series, and while you are there join the Facebook page, so you are first to know when a new book comes out.

Characters

Chorus

King Henry V-Recent crowned king of England.

The Dukes of Exeter, Westmorland, Salisbury, and Warwick-Advisors of King Henry and military leaders.

The Dukes of Clarence, Bedford and Gloucester-Brothers of King Henry

The Archbishop of Canterbury and the Bishop of Ely-English Clergymen

Cambridge, Scroop, and Grey-Conspirators against King Henry.

York and Suffolk-Noble cousins.

The King of France-Charles VI.

Isabel-Queen of France.

The Dauphin-Son of the king of France.

Catherine-Daughter of the king of France.

French noblemen and military leaders-Constable of France, the Duke of Orleans, the Duke of Britain, the Duke of Bourbon, the Earl of Grandpre, Lord Rambures, the Duke of Burgandy, and the Governor of Harfleur.

Sir Thomas Erpingham-War veteran serving King Henry.

Captain Gower-Army Captain.

Captain Fluellen, Captain Macmorris, and Captain Jamy-Captains of King Henry's troops.

Ancient Pistol-London Commoner serving King Henry.

Bardolph-Friend of Pistol.

Nim-London commoner serving King Henry.

Boy

Michael Williams, John Bates, and Alexander Court-Common soldiers.

Hostess-Keeper of the Boar's Head Tavern.

Alice-Maid of Princess Catherine.

Montjoy-French herald.

Monsieur le Fer-French soldier.

Play

Act I

Prologue

Chorus

O for a Muse of fire, that would ascendThe brightest heaven of invention,A kingdom for a stage, princes to act,And monarchs to behold the swelling scene!Then should the warlike Harry, like himself,Assume the port of Mars; and at his heels,Leash'd in like hounds, should famine, sword, and fireCrouch for employment. But pardon, gentles all,The flat unraised spirits that hath dar'dOn this unworthy scaffold to bring forthSo great an object. Can this cockpit holdThe vasty fields of France? Or may we cramWithin this wooden O the very casquesThat did affright the air at Agincourt?O, pardon! since a crooked figure mayAttest in little place a million;And let us, ciphers to this great accompt,On your imaginary forces work.Suppose within the girdle of these wallsAre now confin'd two mighty monarchies,Whose high upreared and abutting frontsThe perilous narrow ocean parts asunder;Piece out our imperfections with your thoughts:Into a thousand parts divide one man,And make imaginary puissance;Think, when we talk of horses, that you see themPrinting their proud hoofs i' the receiving earth.For 'tis your thoughts that now must deck our kings,Carry them here and there, jumping o'er times,Turning the accomplishment of many yearsInto an hour-glass: for the which supply,Admit me Chorus to this history;Who, prologue-like, your humble patience pray,Gently to hear, kindly to judge, our play.

With the help of the Muse of fire, we present a kingdom on a stage where princes will act and kings will hold war. We bring to you the vast fields of France on this small stage to represent the frightening scene of Agincourt. Try to imagine two might monarchies separated by an ocean. Overlook the imperfections and imagine the horses when we talk of them with their proud hooves pounding the earth. Focus on the epic story we have summarized for the sake of time. Listen and judge our play.

Exit.

Scene 1: London. An ante-chamber in the King's palace.

Enter the Archbishop of Canterbury and the Bishop of Ely.

Canterbury
My lord, I'll tell you: that self bill is urg'd,Which in the eleventh year of the last king's reignWas like, and had indeed against us pass'd,But that the scambling and unquiet timeDid push it out of farther question.

I'm afraid that the same bill reviewed in the king's eleventh year of reign is back up. It almost passed, but the time wasn't right.

Ely
But how, my lord, shall we resist it now?

How are we going to get it vetoed this time?

Canterbury
It must be thought on. If it pass against us,We lose the better half of our possession;For all the temporal lands, which men devoutBy testament have given to the Church,Would they strip from us; being valu'd thus:As much as would maintain, to the King's honour,Full fifteen earls and fifteen hundred knights,Six thousand and two hundred good esquires;And, to relief of lazars and weak age,Of indigent faint souls, past corporal toil,A hundred almshouses right well suppli'd;And to the coffers of the King beside,A thousand pounds by the year. Thus runs the bill.

We have to think about it. If it passes, we will lose half of what we own. We would lose enough land given to us by devout men to maintain fifteen earls and fifteen hundred knights, and six thousand two hundred squires, not to mention the upkeep of lepers, old men unable to work, a hundred almshouses, and a thousand pounds to put in the king's bank.

Ely
This would drink deep.

That would really drain us.

Canterbury
'Twould drink the cup and all.

Completely.

Ely
But what prevention?

So, how do we prevent it from passing?

Canterbury
The King is full of grace and fair regard.

The king is fair and full of grace.

Canterbury
The courses of his youth promis'd it not.The breath no sooner left his father's body,But that his wildness, mortifi'd in him,Seem'd to die too; yea, at that very momentConsideration

As soon as his father died, it was like the wildness left his body and was inhabited by an angel. He turned into a scholar and great

like an angel cameAnd whipp'd the offending Adam out of him,Leaving his body as a paradiseTo envelope and contain celestial spirits.Never was such a sudden scholar made;Never came reformation in a floodWith such a heady currance, scouring faults;Nor never Hydra-headed wilfulnessSo soon did lose his seat, and all at once,As in this king.

Ely
We are blessed in the change.

We have been blessed.

Canterbury
Hear him but reason in divinity,And, all-admiring, with an inward wishYou would desire the King were made a prelate;Hear him debate of commonwealth affairs,You would say it hath been all in all his study;List his discourse of war, and you shall hearA fearful battle rend'red you in music;Turn him to any cause of policy,The Gordian knot of it he will unloose,Familiar as his garter; that, when he speaks,The air, a charter'd libertine, is still,And the mute wonder lurketh in men's ears,To steal his sweet and honey'd sentences;So that the art and practic' part of lifeMust be the mistress to this theoric:Which is a wonder how his Grace should glean it,Since his addiction was to courses vain,His companies unletter'd, rude, and shallow,His hours fill'd up with riots, banquets, sports,And never noted in him any study,Any retirement, any sequestrationFrom open haunts and popularity.

If you heard him talk about things pertaining to the church, you would wish he were made a priest. If you heard him debate affairs of the state, you would think he had studied it all his life. If you heard him discuss war, you would hear a lyrical tale of battle. Ask him about any policy, and when he speaks, freedom rings in the air with his sweet sentences. And, who knows where he learned all of it, since he was addicted to worldly habits of riots, parties, and sports. He never studied or practiced quiet contemplation.

Ely
The strawberry grows underneath the nettle,And wholesome berries thrive and ripen bestNeighbour'd by fruit of baser quality;And so the Prince obscur'd his contemplationUnder the veil of wildness; which, no doubt,Grew like the summer grass,
fastest by night,Unseen, yet crescive in his *reformer.*

The best fruit grows underneath weeds, and the most wholesome berries thrive when surrounded by weaker fruit. So, the prince got his ability to think while he was busy with wild activities. No one knew he was mastering these qualities.

faculty.

Canterbury

It must be so; for miracles are ceas'd,And therefore we must needs admit the meansHow things are perfected.

Canterbury

He seems indifferent,Or rather swaying more upon our partThan cherishing the exhibiters against us;For I have made an offer to his Majesty,Upon our spiritual convocationAnd in regard of causes now in hand,Which I have open'd to his Grace at large,As touching France, to give a greater sumThan ever at one time the clergy yetDid to his predecessors part withal.

Ely

How did this offer seem receiv'd, my lord?

Canterbury

With good acceptance of his Majesty;Save that there was not time enough to hear,As I perceiv'd his Grace would fain have done,The severals and unhidden passagesOf his true titles to some certain dukedoms,And generally to the crown and seat of FranceDeriv'd from Edward, his great-grandfather.

Ely

What was the impediment that broke this off?

Canterbury

The French ambassador upon that instantCrav'd audience; and the hour, I think, is comeTo give him hearing. Is it four o'clock?

Ely

It is.

Canterbury

Then go we in, to know his embassy;Which I could with a ready guess declare,Before the Frenchman speak a word of it.

It must be true since there aren't any miracles. Therefore, that would explain things.

He seems indifferent, or he may be swaying towards our opinion. I have made an offer to him concerning France, on our behalf, to give him a large sum, greater than any before.

How did he respond to your offer?

There wasn't a whole lot of time, but he seemed to accept it well, although he would have liked to hear more about how he is entitled to certain dukedoms in France, and even the throne based on his great-grandfather, Edward.

What interrupted the conversation?

The French ambassador requested to be seen. I think it's time to hear him. Is it four o'clock?

Yes, it is.

Then we should go see what he wants. I bet I already know.

Ely
I'll wait upon you, and I long to hear it.   *I can't wait to hear it.*

Exit.

Scene II: The same. The Presence chamber.

Enter King Henry V, Gloucester, Bedford, Exeter, Warwick, Westmoreland, and Attendants.

King

Where is my gracious Lord of Canterbury?

Where is my gracious Lord of Canterbury?

Exeter

Not here in presence.

He is not here.

King

Send for him, good uncle.

Please send for him, uncle.

Westmoreland

Shall we call in the ambassador, my liege?

Do you want us to call in the ambassador, my liege?

King

Not yet, my cousin. We would be resolv'd,Before we hear him, of some things of weightThat task our thoughts, concerning us and France.

Not yet, cousin. We need to be in agreement on some tasks concerning France before we hear him.

Enter the Archbishop of Canterbury and the Bishop of Ely.

Canterbury

God and his angels guard your sacred throneAnd make you long become it!

May God and the angels guard your sacred throne.

King

Sure, we thank you.My learned lord, we pray you to proceedAnd justly and religiously unfoldWhy the law Salique that they have in FranceOr should, or should not, bar us in our claim;And God forbid, my dear and faithful lord,That you should fashion, wrest, or bow your reading,Or nicely charge your understanding soulWith opening titles miscreate, whose rightSuits not in native colours with the truth;For God doth know how many now in healthShall drop their blood in approbationOf what your reverence shall incite us to.Therefore take heed how you impawn our person,How you awake our sleeping sword of war.We charge you, in the name of God, take heed;For never two such blood, whose guiltless dropsAre every one a

Thank you. We ask you to explain the claims we have in France. Tell us truthfully, because only God knows how many will die based on your information. So, be careful how you interpret the law or else create a war. We trust that what you say is true, so speak.

12

woe, a sore complaint'Gainst him whose wrongs gives edge unto the swordsThat makes such waste in brief mortality.Under this conjuration speak, my lord;For we will hear, note, and believe in heartThat what you speak is in your conscience wash'dAs pure as sin with baptism.

Canterbury

Then hear me, gracious sovereign, and you peers,That owe yourselves, your lives, and servicesTo this imperial throne. There is no barTo make against your Highness' claim to FranceBut this, which they produce from Pharamond:"In terram Salicam mulieres ne succedant,""No woman shall succeed in Salique land;"Which Salique land the French unjustly glozeTo be the realm of France, and PharamondThe founder of this law and female bar.Yet their own authors faithfully affirmThat the land Salique is in Germany,Between the floods of Sala and of Elbe;Where Charles the Great, having subdu'd the Saxons,There left behind and settled certain French;Who, holding in disdain the German womenFor some dishonest manners of their life,Establish'd then this law, to wit, no femaleShould be inheritrix in Salique land;Which Salique, as I said, 'twixt Elbe and Sala,Is at this day in Germany call'd Meisen.Then doth it well appear the Salique lawWas not devised for the realm of France;Nor did the French possess the Salique landUntil four hundred one and twenty yearsAfter defunction of King Pharamond,Idly suppos'd the founder of this law,Who died within the year of our redemptionFour hundred twenty-six; and Charles the GreatSubdu'd the Saxons, and did seat the FrenchBeyond the river Sala, in the yearEight hundred five. Besides, their writers say,King Pepin, which deposed Childeric, Did, as heir general, being descendedOf Blithild, which was daughter to King Clothair,Make claim and title to the crown of

Listen, my lord and peers who serve the king. There is nothing to keep us from making a claim in France, except what the law from Pharamond states. It says that no woman shall rule in Salique. The French think Salique is part of France, but it is actually part of Germany. Charles the Great left French settlements after conquering the Saxons, and the French settlers hated the behavior of the German women, so they passed the law. The area is now called Meisen, and the law was not meant for France. France didn't even own the land until after the death of Pharamond in the year 426, so it was not his law. Charles established the settlement in the year 805. According to history, King Pepin, who took the crown from Childeric, based his right on his descendants from, Blithild, the daughter of King Clothair. Another example is Hugh Capet, who stole the crown form Charles the duke of Lorraine, based on his ancestor Lady Lingare, daughter of Charlemagne, the son of Lewis the Emperor, the son of Charles the Great. King Lewis the Tenth, the sole heir to Capet, did not rest until he confirmed his grandmother, Queen Isabel, was a direct descendent of Lady Ermengare, the daughter of Charles duke of Lorraine, reuniting through marriage the line of Charles the Great to the throne. So, it is clear the heir to the throne is directly related to females.

France.Hugh Capet also, who usurp'd the crownOf Charles the Duke of Lorraine, sole heir maleOf the true line and stock of Charles the Great,To find his title with some shows of truth,Though, in pure truth, it was corrupt and naught,Convey'd himself as the heir to the Lady Lingare,Daughter to Charlemain, who was the sonTo Lewis the Emperor, and Lewis the sonOf Charles the Great. Also, King Lewis the Tenth,Who was sole heir to the usurper Capet,Could not keep quiet in his conscience,Wearing the crown of France, till satisfiedThat fair Queen Isabel, his grandmother,Was lineal of the Lady Ermengare,Daughter to Charles, the foresaid Duke of Lorraine;By the which marriage the line of Charles the GreatWas re-united to the crown of France.So that, as clear as is the summer's sun,King Pepin's title and Hugh Capet's claim,King Lewis his satisfaction, all appearTo hold in right and title of the female.So do the kings of France unto this day,Howbeit they would hold up this Salique lawTo bar your Highness claiming from the female,And rather choose to hide them in a netThan amply to imbar their crooked titlesUsurp'd from you and your progenitors.

King
May I with right and conscience make this claim?

Canterbury
The sin upon my head, dread sovereign!For in the book of Numbers is it writ,When the man dies, let the inheritanceDescend unto the daughter. Gracious lord,Stand for your own! Unwind your bloody flag!Look back into your mighty ancestors!Go, my dread lord, to your great-grandsire's tomb,From whom you claim; invoke his warlike spirit,And your great-uncle's, Edward the Black Prince,Who on the French ground play'd a tragedy,Making defeat on the full power of France,Whiles his most mighty father on a hillStood smiling to behold his lion's whelpForage in blood of French

Can I, in good conscience, make this claim?

If you can't, let the sin be with me, for it says in the Bible in the book of Numbers, when a man dies, let the inheritance descend unto the daughter. Gracious lord, make your claim and fly your war flag. Look to your ancestors, your great-grandfather's warring spirit and your great uncle, Edward the Black Prince, who fought a battle on French soil with his father watching on a hill. The noble English can take on the French with only half of their army, while the other half stands by laughing.

nobility.O noble English, that could entertainWith half their forces the full pride of FranceAnd let another half stand laughing by,All out of work and cold for action!

Ely
Awake remembrance of these valiant dead,And with your puissant arm renew their feats.You are their heir; you sit upon their throne;The blood and courage that renowned themRuns in your veins; and my thrice-puissant liegeIs in the very May-morn of his youth,Ripe for exploits and mighty enterprises.

Remember the brave dead for their feats. You share their blood and you sit upon the throne. You are young and ready to fight for what is yours.

Exeter
Your brother kings and monarchs of the earthDo all expect that you should rouse yourself,As did the former lions of your blood.

All the kings of the earth expect you to follow in the footsteps of your ancestors.

Westmoreland
They know your Grace hath cause and means and might;So hath your Highness. Never King of EnglandHad nobles richer, and more loyal subjects,Whose hearts have left their bodies here in EnglandAnd lie pavilion'd in the fields of France.

They know you have cause, the means, and the power. You have financial support and loyal men who are already in France.

Canterbury
O, let their bodies follow, my dear liege,With blood and sword and fire to win your right;In aid whereof we of the spiritualtyWill raise your Highness such a mighty sumAs never did the clergy at one timeBring in to any of your ancestors.

Let the men fight, my liege. We, spiritual men, will provide a greater sum than ever seen by another monarchy.

King
We must not only arm to invade the French,But lay down our proportions to defendAgainst the Scot, who will make road upon usWith all advantages.

We must not only invade France, but also prepare a defense against Scotland, who will definitely attack us.

Canterbury
They of those marches, gracious sovereign,Shall be a wall sufficient to

We will build a wall of defense, oh gracious sovereign, against any who march against us.

defendOur inland from the pilfering borderers.

King
We do not mean the coursing snatchers only,But fear the main intendment of the Scot,Who hath been still a giddy neighbour to us;For you shall read that my great-grandfatherNever went with his forces into FranceBut that the Scot on his unfurnish'd kingdomCame pouring, like the tide into a breach,With ample and brim fullness of his force,Galling the gleaned land with hot assays,Girdling with grievous siege castles and towns;That England, being empty of defence,Hath shook and trembled at the ill neighbourhood.

We don't worry about a few soldiers, but the entire kingdom of Scotland. My great-grandfather never went to war with France that the Scots tried to invade the country while it was defenseless, leaving England shaking with fear.

Canterbury
She hath been then more fear'd than harm'd, my liege;For hear her but exampl'd by herself:When all her chivalry hath been in France,And she a mourning widow of her nobles,She hath herself not only well defendedBut taken and impounded as a strayThe King of Scots; whom she did send to FranceTo fill King Edward's fame with prisoner kings,And make her chronicle as rich with praiseAs is the ooze and bottom of the seaWith sunken wreck and sumless treasuries.

England may have been fearful, but she was never harmed, my liege. We apprehended the King of Scots while the army was in France and sent him there to King Edward. England was praised more than the ooze at the bottom of the sea.

Westmoreland
But there's a saying very old and true,
"If that you will France win,Then with Scotland first begin."For once the eagle England being in prey,To her unguarded nest the weasel ScotComes sneaking and so sucks her princely eggs,Playing the mouse in absence of the cat,To tear and havoc more than she can eat.

Remember the old saying, "When the cat's away, the mice will play." If we win France, we will have to fight Scotland, next.

Exeter
It follows then the cat must stay at home; Yet that is but a crush'd necessity, Since we have locks to safeguard necessaries,
And pretty traps to catch the petty

Then the cat must stay at home. However, that's not necessary, for while the armed hand fights abroad, the head advisors will defend the home. The government, although split into different

abroad,The advised head defends itself at home;For government, though high and low and lower,Put into parts, doth keep in one consent,Congreeing in a full and natural close,Like music.

Canterbury

Therefore doth heaven divideThe state of man in divers functions,Setting endeavour in continual motion,To which is fixed, as an aim or butt,Obedience; for so work the honey-bees,Creatures that by a rule in nature teachThe act of order to a peopled kingdom.They have a king and officers of sorts,Where some, like magistrates, correct at home,Others like merchants, venture trade abroad,Others, like soldiers, armed in their stings,Make boot upon the summer's velvet buds,Which pillage they with merry march bring homeTo the tent-royal of their emperor;Who, busied in his majesty, surveysThe singing masons building roofs of gold,The civil citizens kneading up the honey,The poor mechanic porters crowding inTheir heavy burdens at his narrow gate,The sad-eyed justice, with his surly hum,Delivering o'er to executors paleThe lazy yawning drone. I this infer,That many things, having full referenceTo one consent, may work contrariously.As many arrows, loosed several ways,Come to one mark; as many ways meet in one town;As many fresh streams meet in one salt sea;As many lines close in the dial's centre;So many a thousand actions, once afoot,End in one purpose, and be all well borneWithout defeat. Therefore to France, my liege!Divide your happy England into four,Whereof take you one quarter into France,And you withal shall make all Gallia shake.If we, with thrice such powers left at home,Canot defend our own doors from the dog,Let us be worried and our nation loseThe name of hardiness and policy.

King

degrees, will work together as one like harmonious music.

Heaven created men to have different functions like the honey bees. Honey bees are an example of order. They have a leader with diplomats, judges who correct others, and soldiers armed with stingers who bring home loot to their emperor while he watches his kingdom being built. So, I believe if we work together, we may have success in our common goal. Therefore, my king, divide your armies into four and take a quarter to France. Leave three times that many soldiers at home, and if we can't defend ourselves, we should not call ourselves a nation.

Call in the messengers sent from the Dauphin.

Call in the messengers sent from the Dauphin.

Exit some Attendants.

Now are we well resolv'd; and, by God's help,And yours, the noble sinews of our power,France being ours, we'll bend it to our awe,Or break it all to pieces. Or there we'll sit,Ruling in large and ample emperyO'er France and all her almost kingly dukedoms,Or lay these bones in an unworthy urn,Tombless, with no remembrance over them.Either our history shall with full mouthSpeak freely of our acts, or else our grave,Like Turkish mute, shall have a tongueless mouth,Not worshipp'd with a waxen epitaph.

Now, are we all in agreement. With God's help and the power of you noble men, let's take France. I will defeat France and take rule or you can put my bones in a poor man's urn without a tomb or epitaph for remembrance.

Enter Ambassadors of France

Now are we well prepar'd to know the pleasureOf our fair cousin Dauphin; for we hearYour greeting is from him, not from the King.

We are ready to hear from our cousin, Dauphin, since we hear the greeting is from him, not the king.

First Ambassador
May't please your Majesty to give us leaveFreely to render what we have in charge,Or shall we sparingly show you far offThe Dauphin's meaning and our embassy?

May we have your permission to speak freely?

King
We are no tyrant, but a Christian king,Unto whose grace our passion is as subjectAs is our wretches fett'red in our prisons;Therefore with frank and with uncurbed plainnessTell us the Dauphin's mind.

We are not a group of tyrants. I am a Christian king. Please speak freely and tell us what is on the Dauphin's mind.

First Ambassador
Thus, then, in few.Your Highness, lately sending into France,Did claim some certain dukedoms, in the rightOf your great predecessor, King Edward the Third.
In answer of which claim, the prince our masterSays that you savour too much of your youth,And bids you be advis'd there's nought in FranceThat can be with a nimble galliard

In brief, you sent messages to France stating some claim to certain dukedoms based on your ancestor, King Edward the Third. The answer from our prince is you want too much, and there is nothing you can win in France. He sends you these treasures and asks that you make no more claims.

19

won.You cannot revel into dukedoms there.He therefore sends you, meeter for your spirit,This tun of treasure; and, in lieu of this,Desires you let the dukedoms that you claimHear no more of you. This the Dauphin speaks.

King
What treasure, uncle?

Exeter
Tennis-balls, my liege.

King
We are glad the Dauphin is so pleasant with us.His present and your pains we thank you for.When we have match'd our rackets to these balls,We will, in France, by God's grace, play a setShall strike his father's crown into the hazard.Tell him he hath made a match with such a wranglerThat all the courts of France will be disturb'dWith chaces. And we understand him well,How he comes o'er us with our wilder days,Not measuring what use we made of them.We never valu'd this poor seat of England;And therefore, living hence, did give ourselfTo barbarous licence; as 'tis ever commonThat men are merriest when they are from home.But tell the Dauphin I will keep my state,Be like a king, and show my sail of greatnessWhen I do rouse me in my throne of France.For that I have laid by my majestyAnd plodded like a man for working days,But I will rise there with so full a gloryThat I will dazzle all the eyes of France,Yea, strike the Dauphin blind to look
on us.And tell the pleasant prince this mock of hisHath turn'd his balls to gun-stones, and his soulShall stand sore charged for the wasteful vengeanceThat shall fly with them; for many a thousand widowsShall this his mock mock out of their dear husbands,Mock mothers from their sons, mock castles down;And some are yet ungottenn and unbornThat shall have cause to curse the Dauphin's scorn.But this lies all

What treasure, uncle?

Tennis balls, my liege.

We gladly accept the Dauphin's present and thank you for bringing them. We will have to play a set when we march to France with our rackets. We will strike his father's crown so hard that he will think he has made a match with a professional, and the courts in France will quake. I understand where the Dauphin is coming from, thinking of my wilder days, but I will act like a king when we sail to France, and the people will be amazed while the Dauphin will barely be able to look. Tell the good prince his joke has turned his balls into bullets and he will be sorry for mocking this court when thousands of windows will be made and mothers lose their sons and castles will be torn down. Even the unborn will rue the day he scorned us. However, everything relies on the will of God, upon whose name I call. Tell Dauphin I am coming to claim what is mine. Go in peace and tell him his joke will cause thousands more to weep than those who laughed. Go safely. Goodbye.

within the will of God,To whom I do appeal; and in whose nameTell you the Dauphin I am coming onTo venge me as I may, and to put forthMy rightful hand in a well-hallow'd cause.So get you hence in peace; and tell the DauphinHis jest will savour but of shallow wit,When thousands weep more than did laugh at it.--Convey them with safe conduct.--Fare you well.

Exit Ambassadors.

Exeter
This was a merry message.

That was a happy message.

King
We hope to make the sender blush at it.Therefore, my lords, omit no happy hourThat may give furtherance to our expedition;For we have now no thought in us but France,Save those to God, that run before our business.Therefore, let our proportions for these warsBe soon collected, and all things thought uponThat may with reasonable swiftness addMore feathers to our wings; for, God before,We'll chide this Dauphin at his father's door.Therefore let every man now task his thought,That this fair action may on foot be brought.

I hope it makes his messengers blush. However, let's not waste any time. Our every thought must be of France, except for those that will run our affairs at home. Let's get prepared for war. Collect everything we need so we may leave quickly. We'll correct Dauphin at his father's door. Everyone needs to get to their tasks to make this happen.

Exit. Flourish.

Act II

Prologue

Chorus

Now all the youth of England are on fire,And silken dalliance in the wardrobe lies.Now thrive the armourers, and honour's thoughtReigns solely in the breast of every man.They sell the pasture now to buy the horse,Following the mirror of all Christian kings,With winged heels, as English Mercuries.For now sits Expectation in the air,And hides a sword from hilts unto the pointWith crowns imperial, crowns, and coronets,Promis'd to Harry and his followers.The French, advis'd by good intelligenceOf this most dreadful preparation,Shake in their fear, and with pale policySeek to divert the English purposes.O England! model to thy inward greatness,Like little body with a mighty heart,What mightst thou do, that honour would thee do,Were all thy children kind and natural!But see thy fault!France hath in thee found outA nest of hollow bosoms, which he fillsWith treacherous crowns; and three corrupted men,One, Richard Earl of Cambridge, and the second,Henry Lord Scroop of Masham, and the third,Sir Thomas Grey, knight of Northumberland,Have, for the gilt of France,--O guilt indeed!--Confirm'd conspiracy with fearful France;And by their hands this grace of kings must die,If hell and treason hold their promises,Ere he take ship for France, and in Southampton.Linger your patience on, and we'll digestThe abuse of distance, force a play.The sum is paid; the traitors are agreed;The King is set from London; and the sceneIs now transported, gentles, to Southampton.There is the playhouse now, there must you sit;And thence to France shall we convey you safe,And bring you back, charming the narrow seasTo give you gentle pass; for, if we may,We'll not offend one

Enter Chorus.
Now all the youth of England are on fire with the thoughts of war ahead, selling their land to buy horses. Expectation fills the air, as men prepare for war. The French, with knowledge of England's invasion, shake in fear and try to create policies to divert the English. Oh, England! You are a model of greatness. If only all your children were so kind! But fault lies within three corrupt men, Richard, Earl of Cambridge, Henry, Lord Scroop of Masham, and Sir Thomas Grey, Knight of Northumberland. Oh, treachery and guilt! They conspire with France to bring down the king. Now, please be patient and watch as we perform the play. The sum is paid and the traitors have agreed. The king has left from London and arrived in Southampton. We will take you to France, but we will bring you back without offending your stomach, but not until the king comes. We are now in Southampton.

stomach with our play.But, till the King come forth, and not till then,Unto Southampton do we shift our scene.

Exit.

Scene I: London. A street.

Bardolph
Well met, Corporal Nym.

Welcome, Corporal Nym.

Nym
Good morrow, Lieutenant Bardolph.

Hello, Lieutenant Bardolph.

Bardolph
What, are Ancient Pistol and you friends yet?

Are you and the Ancient Pistol friends, yet?

Nym
For my part, I care not. I say little; but when time shallserve, there shall be smiles; but that shall be as it may. I dare not fight, but I will wink and hold out mine iron. It is a simple one, but what though? It will toast cheese, and it will endure cold as another man's sword will; and there's an end.

I don't care. I say very little, but when the time comes, there will be smiles. I will not fight. I will wink and hold out my sword. It's a simple one, but it will toast cheese, and it will take the cold as well as any other man's.

Bardolph
I will bestow a breakfast to make you friends; and we'llbe all three sworn brothers to France. Let it be so, goodCorporal Nym.

I will hold a breakfast to make you friends and we'll all be three sworn brothers when we travel to France. Is that okay, Corporal Nym?

Nym
Faith, I will live so long as I may, that's the certain of it; and when I cannot live any longer, I will do as I may. That is my rest, that is the rendezvous of it.

I swear, I will live as long as I can. That I am certain of. And, when my time has come, I will do what I want.

Bardolph
It is certain, corporal, that he is married to Nell Quickly; and certainly she did you wrong, for you were troth-plight to her.

It's true, Corporal, that he is married to Nell, and she did you wrong because she was supposed to marry you.

Nym
I cannot tell. Things must be as they may. Men may sleep, and they may have their throats about them at that time; and some say knives have edges. It must be as it may. Though patience be a tired mare, yet she will plod. There must be conclusions. Well, I cannot tell.

I guess so. I am tired of being patient. There must be an end to this, although I don't know when.

Bardolph
Here comes Ancient Pistol and his wife. Good
Corporal, bepatient here. How now, mine host
Pistol!

Pistol
Base tike, call'st thou me host?Now, by this
hand, I swear I scorn the term;Nor shall my Nell
keep lodgers.

Hostess
No, by my troth, not long; for we cannot lodge
and board adozen or fourteen gentlewomen that
live honestly by the prick of their needles, but it
will be thought we keep a bawdy house straight.

O well a day, Lady, if he be not drawn now! We
shall see wilful adultery and murder committed.

Bardolph
Good Lieutenant! good corporal! offer nothing
here.

Nym
Pish!

Pistol
Pish for thee, Iceland dog! thou prick-ear'd cur
of Iceland!

Hostess
Good Corporal Nym, show thy valour, and put
up your sword.

Nym
Will you shog off? I would have you solus.

Pistol
"Solus," egregious dog! O viper vile!The "solus"
in thy most mervailous face;The "solus" in thy
teeth, and in thy throat,And in thy hateful lungs,
yea, in thy maw, perdy,And, which is worse,
within thy nasty mouth!I do
retort the "solus" in thy bowels;For I can take,

Enter Pistol and Hostess.

*Here comes Ancient Pistol and his wife. Be
good, Corporal. Be patient here. How are you
my host, Pistol?*

*Did you call me a host? I am not your host and
my Nell does not keep lodgers.*

*No, honestly, we cannot board twelve or
fourteen women who make a living by sewing
without someone thinking we run a brothel.*

Nym and Pistol draw.

*Oh, he better draw now, or else we will see a
murder and adultery committed today.*

*Good Lieutenant! Good Corporal! Don't do this
here.*

So what!

*So what, you Icelandic dog! You rascal of
Iceland!*

*Good Corporal Nym, show your valor and put
away your sword.*

*Will you go away? I would love to get you
alone.*

*You want to get me alone, you dog? Oh you
snake! The loneliness is in your face, teeth,
throat, and hateful lungs. It's even in your nasty
mouth! I will make your bowels lonely when I
blow them out of your body with my gun.*

25

and Pistol's cock is up,And flashing fire will follow.

Nym
I am not Barbason; you cannot conjure me. I have an humour to knock you indifferently well. If you grow foul with me, Pistol, I will scour you with my rapier, as I may, in fair terms. If you would walk off, I would prick your guts a little, in good terms, as I may; and that's the humour of it.

I am no spirit you can cast spells on. I have a good mind to knock you out. If you get ugly with me, Pistol, I will stab you with my sword. I would prick your guts in all fairness and that would be the end of it.

Pistol
O braggart vile and damned furious wight!The grave doth gape, and doting death is near,Therefore exhale.

You vile man! Your death is near, and your grave is open. Take a deep breath.

Bardolph
Hear me, hear me what I say. He that strikes the firststroke I'll run him up to the hilts, as I am a soldier.

Listen to me. I will kill the person who strikes first. I am a soldier.

Draws.

Pistol
An oath of mickle might; and fury shall abate.Give me thy fist, thy fore-foot to me give.Thy spirits are most tall.

That's a powerful promise. We should calm down. Give me your hand or your foot. You have a brave spirit.

Nym
I will cut thy throat, one time or other, in fair terms:that is the humour of it.

I will cut your throat sooner or later, and that's that.

Pistol
"Couple a gorge!"That is the word. I thee defy again.O hound of Crete, think'st thou my spouse to get?No! to the spital go,And from the powdering tub of infamyFetch forth the lazar kite of Cressid's kind,Doll Tearsheet she by name, and her espouse.I have, and I will hold, the quondam QuicklyFor the only she; and--pauca, there's enough.Go to.

I think you're trying to say, "Couple a gorge!" Do you think you can get my wife? No, go the hospital and get a wife, one with diseases.

Enter the Boy.

Boy
Mine host Pistol, you must come to my master, and you,hostess. He is very sick, and would to

My host, Pistol, you must come to my master. And you, too, hostess. He is very sick and needs

bed. Good Bardolph, put thy face between his sheets, and do the office of a warming-pan. Faith, he's very ill.

help. Good Bardolph, put your face underneath his sheets and be a warming pan. I swear, he is very ill.

Bardolph
Away, you rogue!

Get out of here, you rascal!

Hostess
By my troth, he'll yield the crow a pudding one of these days. The King has kill'd his heart. Good husband, come home presently.

Honestly, he will be food for the crows one day. The king has broken his heart. Come on husband. Come home.

Exit Hostess and Boy.

Bardolph
Come, shall I make you two friends? We must to Francetogether; why the devil should we keep knives to cut oneanother's throats?

Come on. Can't I help you two become friends? We have to go to France together. Should we take our knives to cut each other's throats?

Pistol
Let floods o'erswell, and fiends for food howl on!

Not until the rivers flood and fiends howl for food!

Nym
You'll pay me the eight shillings I won of you at betting?

Are you going to pay me the eight shillings you owe me?

Pistol
Base is the slave that pays.

Only slaves pay debts.

Nym
That now I will have: that's the humour of it.

Then, I will take it now.

Pistol
As manhood shall compound. Push home.

We'll see. Go for it.

They draw.

Bardolph
By this sword, he that makes the first thrust, I'll killhim; by this sword, I will.

I swear by this sword, the first person to make a move, I'll kill.

Pistol
Sword is an oath, and oaths must have their course.

You better be prepared to keep your oath.

Bardolph
Corporal Nym, and thou wilt be friends, be
friends; anthou wilt not, why, then, be enemies
with me too. Prithee,put up.

*If you and Corporal Nym won't be friends, then
you can be my enemies, too. Prepare to fight.*

Nym
I shall have my eight shillings I won from you at
betting?

I just want my eight shillings.

Pistol
A noble shalt thou have, and present pay;And
liquor likewise will I give to thee,And friendship
shall combine, and brotherhood.I'll live by Nym,
and Nym shall live by me.Is not this just? For I
shall sutler beUnto the camp, and profits will
accrue.Give me thy hand.

*Okay, I will pay you, and give you some liquor. I
offer you my hand in friendship, Nym. Give me
your hand.*

Nym
I shall have my noble?

You'll pay me.

Pistol
In cash most justly paid.

Yes, in cash.

Nym
Well, then, that's the humour of't.

Well, then, that's that.

Re-enter Hostess.

Hostess
As ever you come of women, come in quickly to
Sir John.Ah, poor heart! he is so shak'd of a
burning quotidian tertian, that it is most
lamentable to behold. Sweet men, come to him.

*Come as quickly to Sir John as you would to a
woman. Ah, the poor man! He is so feverish, it's
sad to see. Sweet gentlemen, come to him.*

Nym
The King hath run bad humours on the knight;
that's the even of it.

The king has done him wrong. That's that.

Pistol
Nym, thou hast spoke the right.His heart is
fracted and corroborate.

Nym, you are right. His heart is broken.

Nym
The King is a good king; but it must be as it
may; hepasses some humours and careers.

*He is a good king, but be that as it may, he is
fickle.*

Pistol

Let us condole the knight; for, lambkins, we will live.

Let's go see the knight, little lambs, for we will live.

Scene II: Southampton. A council-chamber.

Enter Exeter, Bedford, and Westmoreland.

Bedford
'Fore God, his Grace is bold, to trust these traitors.

I swear before God, the king is bold to trust these traitors.

Exeter
They shall be apprehended by and by.

They will be arrested eventually.

Westmoreland
How smooth and even they do bear themselves! As if allegiance in their bosoms satCrowned with faith and constant loyalty.

They act all smooth, as if they were loyal and faithful men.

Bedford
The King hath note of all that they intend,By interception which they dream not of.

They never expected the king to find out what they were doing.

Exeter
Nay, but the man that was his bed-fellow,Whom he hath dull'd and cloy'd with gracious favours,That he should, for a foreign purse, so sellHis sovereign's life to death and treachery.

No, who would have expected the friend he spoiled would sell his king's life for a little sum of foreign money?

Trumpets sound. Enter King Henry V, Scroop, Cambridge, Grey, and Attendants.

King
Now sits the wind fair, and we will aboard.My Lord of Cambridge, and my kind Lord of Masham,And you, my gentle knight, give me your thoughts.Think you not that the powers we bear with usWill cut their passage through the force of France,Doing the execution and the actFor which we have in head assembled them?

The winds are right for us to sail. My Lord of Cambridge, Lord of Masham, and my gentle knight, tell me what you think. Don't you think the forces we have will be enough to cut through France and achieve our goal?

Scroop
No doubt, my liege, if each man do his best.

King
I doubt not that, since we are well persuadedWe carry not a heart with us from

No doubt, my liege, if every man does his best.

I'm sure everyone will, since we are all in agreement and desire success and conquest.

henceThat grows not in a fair consent with ours,Nor leave not one behind that doth not wishSuccess and conquest to attend on us.

Cambridge

Never was monarch better fear'd and lov'dThan is your Majesty. There's not, I think, a subjectThat sits in heart-grief and uneasinessUnder the sweet shade of your government.

There has never been a king more feared or loved than you. Plus, there's never been an issue before the government wanted more than this.

GREY

True; those that were your father's enemiesHave steep'd their galls in honey, and do serve youWith hearts create of duty and of zeal.

King

We therefore have great cause of thankfulness,And shall forget the office of our handSooner than quittance of desert and meritAccording to the weight and worthiness.

We should be very thankful and remember the importance of our mission.

Scroop

So service shall with steeled sinews toil,And labour shall refresh itself with hope,To do your Grace incessant services.

Every man in your service should work hard and with hope.

King

We judge no less. Uncle of Exeter,Enlarge the man committed yesterday,That rail'd against our person. We considerIt was excess of wine that set him on,And on his more advice we pardon him.

We will accept nothing less. Uncle Exeter, pardon the man who talked poorly about me yesterday. I think he just drank too much.

That's mercy, but too much security.Let him be punish'd, sovereign, lest exampleBreed, by his sufferance, more of such a kind.

That's merciful, but don't be too soft. Let him be punished and set forth as an example or else others may follow suit.

King

O, let us yet be merciful.

Oh, let's be merciful.

CAMBRIDGE

So may your Highness, and yet punish too.

Grey

Sir, You show great mercy if you give him life After the taste of much correction.

Sir, you show him mercy, if you allow him to live after he has been corrected.

King

Alas, your too much love and care of me Are heavy orisons 'gainst this poor wretch! If little faults, proceeding on distemper, Shall not be wink'd at, how shall we stretch our eye When capital crimes, chew'd, swallow'd, and digested, Appear before us? We'll yet enlarge that man, Though Cambridge, Scroop, and Grey, in their dear care And tender preservation of our person, Would have him punish'd. And now to our French causes. Who are the late commissioners?

You love and care for me so much. Don't hold it against this poor man! If we can't overlook such trivial crimes, how are we going to act when faced with capital crimes? Free this man, although Cambridge, Scroop and Grey would like to have him punished. Now, to our French dilemma: Who are the late commissioners?

Cambridge

I one, my lord. Your Highness bade me ask for it to-day.

I am, my lord. You asked me to come today.

Scroop

So did you me, my liege.

Me too, my liege.

Grey

And I, my royal sovereign.

And me, my king.

King

Then, Richard Earl of Cambridge, there is yours; There yours, Lord Scroop of Masham; and, sir knight, Grey of Northumberland, this same is yours. Read them, and know I know your worthiness. My Lord of Westmoreland, and uncle Exeter, We will aboard to-night.--Why, how now, gentlemen! What see you in those papers that you lose So much complexion?-- Look ye, how they change! Their cheeks are paper.--Why, what read you there, That have so cowarded and chas'd your blood Out of appearance?

Then here you go. Read them and know I know you are capable of this. My Lord Westmoreland ad Uncle Exeter, we will leave tonight. Now, gentlemen, what is in those papers that make you so pale? Look at how your faces have turned white as paper. What have you read that has made your blood disappear?

Cambridge

I do confess my fault, And do submit me to your Highness' mercy.

I confess my fault and appeal to your mercy.

Grey and Scroop

To which we all appeal.

King
The mercy that was quick in us but late,By your own counsel is suppress'd and kill'd.You must not dare, for shame, to talk of mercy,For your own reasons turn into your bosoms,As dogs upon their masters, worrying you.
See you, my princes and my noble peers,These English monsters! My Lord of Cambridge here,You know how apt our love was to accordTo furnish him with an appertinentsBelonging to his honour; and this manHath, for a few light crowns, lightly conspir'dAnd sworn unto the practices of FranceTo kill us here in Hampton; to the whichThis knight, no less for bounty bound to usThan Cambridge is, hath likewise sworn. But, OWhat shall I say to thee, Lord Scroop? thou cruel,Ingrateful, savage, and inhuman creature!Thou that didst bear the key of all my counsels,That knew'st the very bottom of my soul,That almost mightst have coin'd me into gold,Wouldst thou have practis'd on me for thy use,--May it be possible that foreign hireCould out of thee extract one spark of evilThat might annoy my finger? 'Tis so strange,That, though the truth of it stands off as grossAs black and white, my eye will scarcely see it.Treason and murder ever kept together,As two yoke-devils sworn to either's purpose,Working so grossly in a natural causeThat admiration did not whoop at them;But thou, 'gainst all proportion, didst bring inWonder to wait on treason and on murder;And whatsoever cunning fiend it wasThat wrought upon thee so preposterouslyHath got the voice in hell for excellence;And other devils that suggest by treasonsDo botch and bungle up damnationWith patches, colours, and with forms being fetch'dFrom glist'ring semblances of piety.But he that temper'd thee bade thee stand up,Gave thee no instance why thou

We all appeal.

Like the mercy you would have shown before. It is too late, and you shouldn't dare talk of mercy. You are like dogs that turn on their masters. See here, my princes and noble peers, the Lord of Cambridge whom we have lavished with honor has sold us out to France for a few little crowns. He swore as well as this knight to kill us here in Hampton. What should I say to you, Lord Scroop? You are a cruel, ungrateful, and inhumane creature! You, who have been the closest to me and knew my heart and soul, would sell me out to murderers. I can barely comprehend it, but here it is in black and white, treason and murder. You have no reason to do this other than to be called a traitor. The devil could walk the entire earth and say, "An Englishman's soul is easy to win." You are infected with jealousy. You seemed serious and educated. You came from a noble family. You seemed religious and pious. You seemed to act justly and judiciously, but here you are fallen. I will cry for you. Arrest them and hold them to the full extent of the law. May God forgive you.

shouldst do treason,Unless to dub thee with the name of traitor.If that same demon that hath gull'd thee thusShould with his lion gait walk the whole world,He might return to vasty Tartar back,And tell the legions, "I can never winA soul so easy as that Englishman's."O, how hast thou with jealousy infectedThe sweetness of affiance! Show men dutiful?Why, so didst thou. Seem they grave and learned?

Why, so didst thou. Come they of noble family?Why, so didst thou. Seem they religious?Why, so didst thou. Or are they spare in diet,Free from gross passion or of mirth or anger,Constant in spirit, not swerving with the blood,Garnish'd and deck'd in modest complement,Not working with the eye without the ear,And but in purged judgement trusting neither?Such and so finely bolted didst thou seem.And thus thy fall hath left a kind of blotTo mark the full-fraught man and best induedWith some suspicion. I will weep for thee;For this revolt of thine, methinks, is likeAnother fall of man. Their faults are open.Arrest them to the answer of the law;And God acquit them of their practices!

Exeter
I arrest thee of high treason, by the name of Richard Earl of Cambridge. I arrest thee of high treason, by the name of Henry Lord Scroop of Masham. I arrest thee of high treason, by the name of Thomas Grey, knight, of Northumberland.

I arrest you and charge you with high treason, Richard Earl of Cambridge, Henry Lord Scroop of Masham, and Thomas Grey, Knight of Northumberland.

Scroop
Our purposes God justly hath discover'd,And I repent my fault more than my death,Which I beseech your Highness to forgive,Although my body pay the price of it.

God has seen fit to reveal our purposes and I repent my actions and pay with my life. I ask you to forgive me.

Cambridge
For me, the gold of France did not seduce,Although I did admit it as a

The gold of France didn't seduce me, although it was a motivation. I am thankful we didn't

motiveThe sooner to effect what I intended.But God be thanked for prevention,Which I in sufferance heartily will rejoice,Beseeching God and you to pardon me.

succeed and I ask God and you to forgive me.

Grey
Never did faithful subject more rejoiceAt the discovery of most dangerous treasonThan I do at this hour joy o'er myself,Prevented from a damned enterprise.My fault, but not my body, pardon, sovereign.

I rejoice at the discovery of this treason and the prevention of such a crime. Please forgive me, king.

King
God quit you in his mercy! Hear your sentence.You have conspir'd against our royal person,Join'd with an enemy proclaim'd, and from his coffersReceived the golden earnest of our death;Wherein you would have sold your king to slaughter,His princes and his peers to servitude,His subjects to oppression and contempt,And his whole kingdom into desolation.Touching our person seek we no revenge;But we our kingdom's safety must so tender,Whose ruin you have sought, that to her lawsWe do deliver you. Get you therefore hence,Poor miserable wretches, to your death,The taste whereof God of his mercy giveYou patience to endure, and true repentanceOf all your dear offences! Bear them hence.

May God have mercy on you! Hear your sentence. You have conspired against this royal throne and joined with an enemy. You have taken the enemy's money and conspired to kill your king, place his princes and peers in servitude, and oppress his subjects to live in desolation. We do not seek revenge, but hold you to the law of our kingdom. Go, you poor miserable wretches, to your death and may God have mercy and give you patience to endure and truly repent all of your offences. Take them away.

Exit Cambridge, Scroop, and Grey guarded.

Now, lords, for France; the enterprise whereofShall be to you, as us, like glorious.We doubt not of a fair and lucky war,Since God so graciously hath brought to lightThis dangerous treason lurking in our wayTo hinder our beginnings. We doubt not nowBut every rub is smoothed on our way.Then forth, dear countrymen! Let us deliverOur puissance into the hand of God,Putting it straight in expedition.Cheerly to sea! The signs of war advance!No king of England, if not king of France!

Now, lords, as for France, I am sure we will be victorious, since God saw fit to bring this treachery to light. We should have no more trouble here on out. Let's put ourselves in God's hands and set sail for France.

Exit.

Scene III: London. Before a tavern.

Enter Pistol, Hostess, Nym, Bardolph, and Boy.

Hostess

Prithee, honey, sweet husband, let me bring thee to Staines.

Let me go with you to Staines, dear husband.

Pistol

No; for my manly heart doth yearn.Bardolph, be blithe; Nym, rouse thy vaunting veins;Boy, bristle thy courage up; for Falstaff he is dead,And we must yearn therefore.

No, because Falstaff is dead. Bardolph, Nym, Boy prepare yourselves.

Bardolph

Would I were with him, wheresome'er he is, either inheaven or in hell!

I wish I was with him, in heaven or hell.

Hostess

Nay, sure, he's not in hell. He's in Arthur's bosom, if ever man went to Arthur's bosom. 'A made a finer end and wentaway an it had been any christom child. 'A parted even just between twelve and one, even at the turning o' the tide: for after I saw him fumble with the sheets, and play with flowers, and smile upon his fingers' ends, I knew there was but one way; for his nose was as sharp as a pen, and 'a babbled of green fields. "How now, Sir John!" quoth I; "what, man! be o' good cheer." So 'a cried out, "God, God, God!" three or four times. Now I, to comfort him, bid him 'a should not think of God; I hop'd there was no need to trouble himself with any such thoughts yet. So 'a bade me lay more clothes on his feet. I put my hand into the bed and felt them, and they were as cold as any stone; then I felt to his knees, [and they were as cold as any stone;] and so upward and upward, and all was as cold as any stone.

I'm sure he's not in hell. He was a christened as a child and in the end he babbled on and cried out to God. I tried to tell him not to think of God, and then he asked me to put more clothes on him. From his feet on up, he was cold as stone.

Nym

They say he cried out of sack.

They say he cried about alcohol.

Hostess

Ay, that 'a did.

Yes.

Bardolph

And of women.

Hostess

Nay, that 'a did not.

Boy

Yes, that 'a did; and said they were devils incarnate.

Hostess

'A could never abide carnation; 'twas a colour he never liked.

Boy

'A said once, the devil would have him about women.

Hostess

'A did in some sort, indeed, handle women; but then he wasrheumatic, and talk'd of the whore of Babylon.

Boy

Do you not remember, 'a saw a flea stick upon Bardolph's nose, and 'a said it was a black soul burning in hell-fire?

Bardolph

Well, the fuel is gone that maintain'd that fire. That's all the riches I got in his service.

Nym

Shall we shog? The King will be gone from Southampton.

Pistol

Come, let's away. My love, give me thy lips.Look to my chattels and my movables.Let senses rule; the word is "Pitch and Pay."Trust none;For oaths are straws, men's faiths are wafer-cakesAnd hold-fast is the only dog, my duck;Therefore, Caveto be thy counsellor.Go, clear thy crystals. Yoke-fellows in arms,Let us to France; like horse-leeches, my boys,To suck, to suck, the very

And he asked for women.

No, he didn't do that.

Yes, he did, and he said they were reincarnated devils.

He never would bear carnations. He didn't like the color.

He said the devil would get him due to women.

He did say something about women, mostly the whore of Babylon, but he was feverish.

Do you remember when he saw a flea on Bardolph's nose and he said it was a black soul burning in hell?

Well, the fuel that burned that fire is gone. That's about all I ever got from him, was a drink.

Should we get going? The king will be gone from Southampton.

Let's go. Kiss me, my love. Look after my property and possessions. Use common sense, and the rule is "Everyone must pay." Don't trust anyone, because oaths are as easily broken as straws. Men's faith is broken as easily as wafers, so the only thing you can trust is what you can hold in your hand, my love. Go dry your eyes. Fellows-in-arms, let's go to France and be like leeches, sucking their blood!

blood to suck!

Boy
And that's but unwholesome food, they say.

That's not wholesome food, they say.

Pistol
Touch her soft mouth, and march.

Kiss her so we can leave.

Bardolph
Farewell, hostess.

Goodbye, hostess.

Kissing her.

Nym
I cannot kiss; that is the humour of it; but, adieu.

I can't kiss anymore, and that's that, but oh well. Goodbye.

Pistol
Let housewifery appear. Keep close, I thee command.

Be careful and stay true, I command you.

Hostess
Farewell; adieu.

Goodbye, farewell.

Exit.

38

Scene IV: France. The King's Palace.

Flourish. Enter the French King, the Dauphin, the Dukes of Berri and Bretagne, the Constable, and Others.

French King

Thus comes the English with full power upon us,And more than carefully it us concernsTo answer royally in our defences.Therefore the Dukes of Berri and of Bretagne,Of Brabant and of Orleans, shall make forth,And you, Prince Dauphin, with all swift dispatch,To line and new repair our towns of warWith men of courage and with means defendant;For England his approaches makes as fierceAs waters to the sucking of a gulf.It fits us then to be as providentAs fears may teach us out of late examplesLeft by the fatal and neglected EnglishUpon our fields.

Therefore, the English are coming with all of their forces. So, we must answer them with our defenses. Dukes of Berri and Bretagne, and Brabant and Orleans, quickly prepare our defense with courageous men. England is a fierce enemy and we must be ready. We can't delay, as we have before and neglect the English in our fields.

Dauphin

My most redoubted father,It is most meet we arm us 'gainst the foe;For peace itself should not so dull a kingdom,Though war nor no known quarrel were in question,But that defences, musters, preparations,Should be maintain'd, assembled, and collected,As were a war in expectation.Therefore, I say, 'tis meet we all go forthTo view the sick and feeble parts of France.And let us do it with no show of fear;No, with no more than if we heard that EnglandWere busied with a Whitsun morris-dance;For, my good liege, she is so idly king'd,Her sceptre so fantastically borneBy a vain, giddy, shallow, humorous youth,That fear attends her not.

My fearsome father, we definitely have to arm ourselves against the enemy even in times of peace. We can't let our guard down. I think we should go visit the weakest areas of France, but show no fear in the process, as if England were just performing a dance. England, my dear king, has a poor leader. Her monarchy is so vain, shallow, silly, and young, that we needn't fear.

Constable

O peace, Prince Dauphin!You are too much mistaken in this king.Question your Grace the late ambassadorsWith what great state he heard their embassy,How well supplied with noble counsellors,How modest in exception, and withalHow terrible in constant resolution,And you shall find his vanities forespentWere but the outside of the Roman

Oh no, Prince Dauphin! I think you are mistaken about this king. Ask the ambassadors who just came back about how noble and competent his counselors are. You'll find out he has reason to be vain, and he hides his discretion within his youth, like gardeners who cover up delicate roots with mulch.

Brutus,Covering discretion with a coat of folly;As gardeners do with ordure hide those rootsThat shall first spring and be most delicate.

Dauphin

Well, 'tis not so, my Lord High Constable;But though we think it so, it is no matter.In cases of defence 'tis best to weighThe enemy more mighty than he seems,So the proportions of defence are fill'd;Which, of a weak and niggardly projection,Doth, like a miser, spoil his coat with scantingA little cloth.

I don't think so, my lord Constable. However, it doesn't matter, because we need to be prepared to fight regardless of the enemy's strength. So, we know what we must do.

French King

Think we King Harry strong;And, Princes, look you strongly arm to meet him.The kindred of him hath been flesh'd upon us;And he is bred out of that bloody strainThat haunted us in our familiar paths. Witness our too much memorable shameWhen Cressy battle fatally was struck,And all our princes captiv'd by the handOf that black name, Edward, Black Prince of Wales;Whiles that his mountain sire, on mountain standing,Up in the air, crown'd with the golden sun,Saw his heroical seed, and smil'd to see him,Mangle the work of nature and defaceThe patterns that by God and by French fathersHad twenty years been made. This is a stemOf that victorious stock; and let us fearThe native mightiness and fate of him.

We should perceive Harry as a strong threat, and arm ourselves accordingly. His ancestors were a bloody line and he is made from the same cloth. Remember the embarrassment, when Edward the Black Prince of Wales captured all of our princes, while his father watched from a hilltop. History designed by God and our French fathers has been in the making the last twenty years, and here he is. Let us fear him and be ready.

Messenger

Ambassadors from Harry King of EnglandDo crave admittance to your Majesty.

Enter a Messenger.

Ambassadors from King Harry of England wish to have word with you, your majesty.

French King

We'll give them present audience. Go, and bring them.

Bring them in. We will see them now.

You see this chase is hotly follow'd, friends.

Exit Messenger and certain Lords.

Dauphin

The chase begins, friends.

Turn head and stop pursuit; for coward dogsMost spend their mouths when what they seem to threatenRuns far before them. Good my sovereign,Take up the English short, and let them knowOf what a monarchy you are the head.Self-love, my liege, is not so vile a sinAs self-neglecting.

Stop pursuing and face them. Cowardly dogs always yell louder when the prey is far off. My good king, show the English what this monarch is made of. Self-love, my liege, is not as bad as self-neglect.

Re-enter Lords, with Exeter and train.

French King
From our brother of England?

Are you from our brother England?

Exeter
From him; and thus he greets your Majesty:He wills you, in the name of God Almighty,That you divest yourself, and lay apartThe borrowed glories that by gift of heaven,By law of nature and of nations, longsTo him and to his heirs; namely, the crownAnd all wide-stretched honours that pertainBy custom and the ordinance of timesUnto the crown of France. That you may know'Tis no sinister nor no awkward claimPick'd from the worm-holes of long-vanish'd days,Nor from the dust of old oblivion rak'd,He sends you this most memorable line,In every branch truly demonstrative;Willing you overlook this pedigree;And when you find him evenly deriv'd From his most fam'd of famous ancestors,Edward the Third, he bids you then resignYour crown and kingdom, indirectly heldFrom him, the native and true challenger.

Yes, and he sends his greetings. He wishes you to relinquish the crown and all the properties and customs associated with the realm of France that is rightly his. He wants you to know this is not a claim of vengeance or vanity. He wants you to know he is the rightful heir of Edward the Third, and based on this information, you should resign your crown and kingdom.

French King
Or else what follows?

And, if I don't?

Exeter
Bloody constraint; for if you hide the crownEven in your hearts, there will he rake for it.Therefore in fierce tempest is he coming,In thunder and in earthquake, like a Jove,That, if requiring fail, he will compel;And bids you, in the bowels of the Lord,Deliver up the crown, and to take

If you don't, he will declare war. He is coming with his army, like a storm or a god, and he wants you to give up the crown and spare the men who will certainly die in the war. This is his message, the same one he gave to Dauphin.

mercyOn the poor souls for whom this hungry warOpens his vasty jaws; and on your headTurning the widows' tears, the orphans' cries,The dead men's blood, the pining maidens' groans,For husbands, fathers, and betrothed lovers,That shall be swallowed in this controversy.This is his claim, his threat'ning, and my message;Unless the Dauphin be in presence here,To whom expressly I bring greeting too.

French King
For us, we will consider of this further.To-morrow shall you bear our full intentBack to our brother of England.

We must consider this. Tomorrow, we will let you know what we are going to do.

Dauphin
For the Dauphin,I stand here for him. What to him from England?

What does the king say about me?

Exeter
Scorn and defiance. Slight regard, contempt,And anything that may not misbecomeThe mighty sender, doth he prize you at.Thus says my king: an if your father's HighnessDo not, in grant of all demands at large,Sweeten the bitter mock you sent his Majesty,He'll call you to so hot an answer of itThat caves and womby vaultages of FranceShall chide your trespass and return your mockIn second accent of his ordinance.

He has nothing to say but scorn and defiance. After the gift you brought, he will call you to answer for your father's decision, so that all of France will turn its back on you and laugh.

Dauphin
Say, if my father render fair return,It is against my will; for I desireNothing but odds with England. To that end,As matching to his youth and vanity,I did present him with the Paris balls.

If my father accepts the king's demands, know it is against my will. I want nothing to do with England. I gave him a gift matching his youth and vanity.

Exeter
He'll make your Paris Louvre shake for it,Were it the mistress-court of mighty Europe;And, be assur'd, you'll find a difference,As we his subjects have in wonder found,Between the promise of his greener

He'll make the Parisian Louvre shake for it, too. You will find a great difference from the man he used to be and who he is now. You will regret it if he stays in France.

daysAnd these he masters now. Now he weighs timeEven to the utmost grain. That you shall readIn your own losses, if he stay in France.

French King
To-morrow shall you know our mind at full.

You will hear my decision tomorrow.

Exeter
Dispatch us with all speed, lest that our kingCome here himself to question our delay;For he is footed in this land already.

Let us know quickly or else the king will come here to find out what's keeping us so long.

FRENCH KING
You shall be soon dispatch'd with fair conditions.A night is but small breath and little pauseTo answer matters of this consequence.

Flourish. Exit.

Act III

Prologue

Enter Chorus

Chorus

Thus with imagin'd wing our swift scene flies,In motion of no less celerityThan that of thought. Suppose that you have seenThe well-appointed king at [Hampton] pierEmbark his royalty, and his brave fleetWith silken streamers the young Phoebus fanning.Play with your fancies; and in them beholdUpon the hempen tackle ship-boys climbing;Hear the shrill whistle which doth order giveTo sounds confus'd; behold the threaden sails,Borne with the invisible and creeping wind,Draw the huge bottoms through the furrow'd sea,Breasting the lofty surge. O, do but thinkYou stand upon the rivage and beholdA city on the inconstant billows dancing;For so appears this fleet majestical,Holding due course to Harfleur. Follow, follow!Grapple your minds to sternage of this navy,And leave your England, as dead midnight still,Guarded with grandsires, babies, and old women,Either past or not arriv'd to pith and puissance.For who is he, whose chin is but enrich'dWith one appearing hair, that will not followThese cull'd and choice-drawn cavaliers to France?Work, work your thoughts, and therein see a siege;Behold the ordnance on their carriages,With fatal mouths gaping on girded Harfleur.Suppose the ambassador from the French comes back,Tells Harry that the King doth offer himKatharine his daughter, and with her, to dowry,Some petty and unprofitable dukedoms.The offer likes not; and the nimble gunnerWith linstock now the devilish cannon touches,

[Alarum, and chambers go off.]

With your imagination see the king depart with his brave fleet from Hampton pier. Look at the men working on the ship and hear the whistle of orders being given as the sails open up to the creeping wind, pulling the huge ship through the sea. Although this looks like a city dancing in the wind, it is a navy leaving England for France. Imagine the ambassador returns from France with the offer of Katherine, the king's daughter, as a dowry for the dukedoms. Since, the King does not like the offer, he prepares for battle. Imagine and watch our performance.

And down goes all before them. Still be
kind,And eke out our performance with your
mind.

Exit.

Scene I: France. Before Harfleur.

King

Once more unto the breach, dear friends, once more,Or close the wall up with our English dead.In peace there's nothing so becomes a manAs modest stillness and humility;But when the blast of war blows in our ears,Then imitate the action of the tiger;Stiffen the sinews, summon up the blood,Disguise fair nature with hard-favour'd rage;Then lend the eye a terrible aspect;Let it pry through the portage of the headLike the brass cannon; let the brow o'erwhelm itAs fearfully as does a galled rockO'erhang and jutty his confounded base,Swill'd with the wild and wasteful ocean.Now set the teeth and stretch the nostril wide,Hold hard the breath, and bend up every spiritTo his full height. On, on, you noblest English,Whose blood is fet from fathers of war-proof!Fathers that, like so many Alexanders,Have in these parts from morn till even fought,And sheath'd their swords for lack of argument.Dishonour not your mothers; now attestThat those whom you call'd fathers did beget you.Be copy now to men of grosser blood,And teach them how to war. And you, good yeomen,Whose limbs were made in England, show us hereThe mettle of your pasture; let us swearThat you are worth your breeding, which I doubt not;For there is none of you so mean and base,That hath not noble lustre in your eyes.I see you stand like greyhounds in the slips,Straining upon the start. The game's afoot!Follow your spirit, and upon this chargeCry, "God for Harry! England and Saint George!"

Let's try one more time, dear friends, to scale the wall or else die trying. In peace, nothing is so becoming a man as stillness and humility, but in times of war, he should imitate the actions of tiger and rage upon the enemy. Open up your senses and fight like your warring English ancestors. Show us what you are made of and honor your mothers and fathers. Good seamen, show your noble nature as we set forth. The time is now. Follow your heart and on command cry, "God for Harry, England, and Saint George!"

Scene II: The same.

Enter Nym, Bardolph, Pistol, and Boy.

Bardolph
On, on, on, on, on! To the breach, to the breach!

On, on, on! To the wall! To the wall!

Nym
Pray thee, corporal, stay. The knocks are too hot; and, for mine own part, I have not a case of lives. The humour of it is too hot; that is the very plain-song of it.

I beg you, corporal, not to go. It's too dangerous. I, myself, don't have enough lives to spare, and that's that.

Pistol
The plain-song is most just, for humours do abound."Knocks go and come; God's vassals drop and die;
And sword and shield,In bloody field,Doth win immortal fame."

That's true, but danger comes and goes. Men live and die, but with their sword and shield in battle, they win immortal fame.

Boy
Would I were in an alehouse in London! I would give all myfame for a pot of ale and safety.

I wish I was in an alehouse in London. I would trade all of the fame for a beer and safety.

Pistol
And I."If wishes would prevail with me,My purpose should not fail with me,
But thither would I hie."

And if I had my wishes, I would not fail, but live.

Boy
"As duly, but not as truly,
As bird doth sing on bough."

True, but not possible.

Enter Fluellen.

Fluellen
Up to the breach, you dogs! Avaunt, you cullions!

Up to the wall, you dogs! Forward, you scumbags!

Driving them forward.

Pistol
Be merciful, great Duke, to men of mould.Abate thy rage, abate thy manly
rage,Abate thy rage, great Duke!Good bawcock, bate thy rage; use lenity, sweet chuck!

Be merciful, great duke, to old men. Calm down. Go easy, dear man.

Nym

These be good humours! Your honour wins bad humours.

This is nonsense. Honor is unhealthy, if you ask me.

Exit all but Boy.

Boy

As young as I am, I have observ'd these three swashers. I am boy to them all three; but all they three, though they would serve me, could not be man to me; for indeed three such antics do not amount to a man. For Bardolph, he is white-liver'd and red-fac'd; by the means whereof 'a faces it out, but fights not. For Pistol, he hath a killing tongue and a quiet sword; by the means whereof 'a breaks words, and keeps whole weapons. For Nym, he hath heard that men of few words are the best men; and therefore he scorns to say his prayers, lest 'a should be thought a coward. But his few bad words are match'd with as few good deeds; for 'a never broke any man's head but his own, and that was against a post when he was drunk. They will steal anything, and call it purchase. Bardolph stole a lute-case, bore it twelve leagues, and sold it for three half-pence. Nym and Bardolph are sworn brothers in filching, and in Calais they stole a fire-shovel. I knew by that piece of service the men would carry coals. They would have me as familiar with men's pockets as their gloves or their handkerchers; which makes much against my manhood, if I should take from another's pocket to put into mine; for it is plain pocketing up of wrongs. I must leave them, and seek some better service. Their villainy goes against my weak stomach, and therefore I must cast it up.

As young as I am, I have watched these three fools. I am their servant, their man, but if it was the other way around, none could be considered a man. Bardolph is a lily-livered, red-faced coward. Pistol is all talk, and Nym, who thinks quiet men are best and won't even say his prayers for fear someone would think he were a coward, has never hurt anyone but himself when he busted his drunken head against a post. They are thieves and liars. Bardolph stole a lute case, carried it for miles and sold it for three half pence. Nym and Bardolph are sworn brothers in thievery. In Calais, they stole a fire shovel, which I knew wasn't theirs. They want me to get into the business, so I must leave them and find someone better to serve. Their villainous ways makes me sick.

Exit.

Gower

Captain Fluellen, you must come presently to the mines. The Duke of Gloucester would speak with you.

Re-enter Fluellen with Gower following.

Captain Fluellen, you must come to the mines now. The Duke of Gloucester wants to speak with you.

Fluellen

To the mines! Tell you the Duke, it is not so good to cometo the mines; for, look you, the mines is not according to the disciplines of the war. The concavities of it is not sufficient; for, look you, the athversary, you may discuss unto the Duke, look you, is digt himself four yard under the countermines. By Cheshu, I think 'a will plow up all, if there is not better directions.

To the mines! Tell the Duke it's not a good idea to go the mines. It goes against the disciplines of war. It's not a good place to fight the adversary. The French are already there and it will not work, by God.

Gower

The Duke of Gloucester, to whom the order of the siege isgiven, is altogether directed by an Irishman, a very valiant gentleman, i' faith.

The Duke of Gloucester, who is in command, is being led by an Irishman, a very gallant fellow.

Fluellen

It is Captain Macmorris, is it not?

Is it Captain Macmorris?

Gower

I think it be.

I think so.

Fluellen

By Cheshu, he is an ass, as in the world. I will verify asmuch in his beard. He has no more directions in the truedisciplines of the wars, look you, of the Roman disciplines, than is a puppy-dog.

By god, he is an ass. He doesn't know anything about the tactics of war.

Enter Macmorris and Captain Jamy

Gower

Here 'a comes; and the Scots captain, Captain Jamy, with him.

Here he comes with Captain Jamy of the Scots.

Fluellen

Captain Jamy is a marvellous falorous gentleman, that iscertain; and of great expedition and knowledge in the aunchient wars, upon my particular knowledge of his directions. By Cheshu, he will maintain his argument as well as any military man in the world, in the disciplines of the pristine wars of the Romans.

Captain Jamy is a great gentleman for sure and very knowledgeable of the ways of war. By God, he will know what to do.

Jamy

I say gud-day, Captain Fluellen.

Good day, Captain Fluellen.

Fluellen

God-den to your worship, good Captain James.

Hello, Captain James.

Gower
How now, Captain Macmorris! have you quit the mines?Have the pioneers given o'er?

How are you, Captain Macmorris? Have you forgotten about the mines? Have the men given up?

Macmorris
By Chrish, la! 'tish ill done! The work ish give over, thetrompet sound the retreat. By my hand I swear, and myfather's soul, the work ish ill done; it ish give over. I would have blowed up the town, so Chrish save me, la! in an hour. O, 'tish ill done, 'tish ill done; by my hand, 'tish ill done!

Christ, it's horrible. The work is done and the trumpet sounded for retreat. I swear the work was not done well. I could have blown up the town in an hour, I swear, but the work wasn't done.

Fluellen
Captain Macmorris, I beseech you now, will you voutsafe me, look you, a few disputations with you, as partly touching or concerning the disciplines of the war, the Roman wars, in the way of argument, look you, and friendly communication; partly to satisfy my opinion, and partly for the satisfaction, look you, of my mind, as touching the direction of the military discipline; that is the point.

Captain Macmorris, I would like to talk with you about war tactics, particularly the Roman's, to see if we agree.

Jamy
It sall be vary gud, gud feith, gud captains bath: and I sall quit you with gud leve, as I may pick occasion; that sall I, marry.

That would be good, good captains. As soon as I have time, we will discuss it.

Macmorris
It is no time to discourse, so Chrish save me. The day is hot, and the weather, and the wars, and the King, and the Dukes. It is no time to discourse. The town is beseech'd, and the trumpet call us to the breach, and we talk, and, be Chrish, do nothing. 'Tis shame for us all. So God sa' me, 'tis shame to stand still; it is shame, by my hand; and there is throats to be cut, and works to be done; and there ish nothing done, so Chrish sa' me, la!

This is no time for a discussion. Christ, save me. The day is hot and war is all around us. It's no time to have a conversation. The town is under raid and the battle trumpet is calling and we sit here talking. Shame on us. God save me. It's a shame to stand still when there are throats to be cut and work to be done.

Jamy
By the mess, ere theise eyes of mine take

I swear before I sleep, I'll do some good work.

themselves to slomber, I'll de gud service, or I'll lig i' the grund for it; ay, or go to death; and I'll pay't as valorously as I may, that sall I suerly do, that is the breff and the long. Marry, I wad full fain heard some question 'tween you tway.

today or die trying, and that's the truth. I would love to hear you two discuss warfare, though

Fluellen

Captain Macmorris, I think, look you, under your correction, there is not many of your nation--

Captain Macmorris, I think there aren't many from your nation...

Macmorris

Of my nation! What ish my nation? Ish a villain, and a bastard, and a knave, and a rascal? What ish my nation? Who talks of my nation?

My nation! What is my nation? You are a villain and a rascal. Who talks about my nation?

Fluellen

Look you, if you take the matter otherwise than is meant, Captain Macmorris, peradventure I shall think you do not use me with that affability as in discretion you ought to use me, look you, being as good a man as yourself, both in the disciplines of war, and in the derivation of my birth, and in other particularities.

Look you, if you take what I'm saying wrong, Captain Macmorris, you don't know me very well. I am as good a man as you, by birth and the disciplines of war.

Macmorris

I do not know you so good a man as myself. So Chrish save me, I will cut off your head.

I know no such thing, so by Christ, I will cut off your head.

Gower

Gentlemen both, you will mistake each other.

Gentlemen, you both are out of line.

Jamy

Ah! that's a foul fault.

And that's a serious fault.

A trumpet sounds.

Gower

The town sounds a parley.

The town is sounding the trumpet.

Fluellen

Captain Macmorris, when there is more better opportunity to be required, look you, I will be so bold as to tell you I know the disciplines of war; and there is an end.

Captain Macmorris, when there is a better time, I will show you I know more about warfare, and that's all.

Exit.

Scene III: The same. Before the gates.

The Governor and some Citizens on the walls; the English forces below. Enter King Henry and his train.

King

How yet resolves the governor of the town?This is the latest parle we will admit;Therefore to our best mercy give yourselves,Or like to men proud of destructionDefy us to our worst; for, as I am a soldier,A name that in my thoughts becomes me best,If I begin the battery once again,I will not leave the half-achieved HarfleurTill in her ashes she lie buried.The gates of mercy shall be all shut up,And the flesh'd soldier, rough and hard of heart,In liberty of bloody hand shall rangeWith conscience wide as hell, mowing like grassYour fresh fair virgins and your flow'ring infants.What is it then to me, if impious War, Array'd in flames like to the prince of fiends,Do with his smirch'd complexion all fell featsEnlink'd to waste and desolation?What is't to me, when you yourselves are cause,If your pure maidens fall into the handOf hot and forcing violation?What rein can hold licentious wickednessWhen down the hill he holds his fierce career?We may as bootless spend our vain commandUpon the enraged soldiers in their spoilAs send precepts to the leviathanTo come ashore. Therefore, you men of Harfleur,Take pity of your town and of your people,Whiles yet my soldiers are in my command,Whiles yet the cool and temperate wind of graceO'erblows the filthy and contagious cloudsOf heady murder, spoil, and villainy.If not, why, in a moment look to seeThe blind and bloody soldier with foul handDefile the locks of your shrill-shrieking daughters;Your fathers taken by the silver beards,And their most reverend heads dash'd to the walls;Your naked infants spitted upon pikes,Whiles the mad mothers with their howls confus'dDo break the clouds, as did the

How does the governor of the town want to resolve this? This is his last chance before I turn my men loose and let them do their worst. I am a soldier, and if I start to fight again, I will not stop until the town of Harfleur is ashes. The gates of mercy will be closed and my soldiers will have their way with your women and children. What is it to me, if in the battles of war, there is complete and utter destruction? What is it to me when you brought all of this on yourselves?

Why do I care if your maidens are violated and what can rein in wickedness once it is loose? Who can stop the blood-thirsty soldiers in the midst of their looting? Therefore, you men of Harfleur, take pity on your town and your people, while I still have command of my soldiers. If you don't give up, you will see bloody soldiers defile your shrieking daughters and old men killed. Your children will be placed upon pikes while their mothers how. Give up like the Jewish women during Herod's bloody slaughter. What do you say? Will you yield and avoid catastrophe or will you continue and be destroyed?

wives of JewryAt Herod's bloody-hunting slaughtermen.What say you? Will you yield, and this avoid,Or, guilty in defence, be thus destroy'd?

Governor
Our expectation hath this day an end.The Dauphin, whom of succours we entreated,Returns us that his powers are yet not readyTo raise so great a siege. Therefore, great King,We yield our town and lives to thy soft mercy.Enter our gates; dispose of us and ours;For we no longer are defensible.

Our hope and expectations have been dashed, because the Dauphin is not ready to send his powers to help us, so we yield our town and lives to you. Be merciful and enter our gates we can no longer defend.

King
Open your gates. Come, uncle Exeter,Go you and enter Harfleur; there remain,And fortify it strongly 'gainst the French.Use mercy to them all. For us, dear uncle,The winter coming on, and sickness growingUpon our soldiers, we will retire to Calais.To-night in Harfleur will we be your guest;To-morrow for the march are we addrest.

Open your gates. Come, Uncle Exeter, enter Harfleur and stay to fortify it against the French. Be merciful, dear uncle, because winter is coming and sickness grows among our soldiers. We will go to Calais tomorrow, but tonight we will stay in Harfleur.

Flourish. The King and his train enter the town.

Scene IV: The French King's palace.

Enter Katharine and Alice.

Katharine
Alice, tu as ete en Angleterre, et tu parles bien le langage.

Alice, you have been to England and know the language.

Alice
Un peu, madame.

A little, madam.

Katharine
Je te prie, m'enseignez; il faut que j'apprenne a parler.Comment appelez-vous la main en Anglois?

Please teach me. I must learn English. What is the word for "la main?"

Alice
La main? Elle est appelee de hand.

"La main?" That is the hand.

Katharine
De hand. Et les doigts?

The hand. What about "les doigts?"

Alice
Les doigts? Ma foi, j'oublie les doigts; mais je mesouviendrai. Les doigts? Je pense qu'ils sont appeles defingres; oui, de fingres.

Les doigts? Goodness, I have forgotten. Let me think. I believe it is fingers. Yes, it is fingers.

Katharine
La main, de hand; les doigts, de fingres. Je pense queje suis le bon ecolier; j'ai gagne deux mots d'Angloisvitement. Comment appelez-vous les ongles?

La main is hand and les doigts is fingers. I am a very good student. I know two words already. What is the word for "les ongles?"

Alice
Les ongles? Nous les appelons de nails.

"Les ongles?" That is nails.

Katharine
De nails. Ecoutez; dites-moi, si je parle bien: de hand,de fingres, et de nails.

Nails. Listen, am I saying it right? Hand, fingers, nails.

Alice
C'est bien dit, madame; il est fort bon Anglois.

Good job, madam. You speak English.

Katharine
Dites-moi l'Anglois pour le bras.

Tell me the English word for "le bras."

Alice
De arm, madame.

Arm, madam.

Katharine
Et le coude?

And "le coud?"

Alice
D'elbow.

The elbow.

Katharine
D'elbow. Je m'en fais la repetition de tous les motsque vous m'avez appris des a present.

Elbow. Let me practice all the words you've taught me.

Alice
Il est trop difficile, madame, comme je pense.

It may be too difficult.

Katharine
Excusez-moi, Alice; ecoutez: d'hand, de fingres, denails, d'arma, de bilbow.

I don't think so, Alice. Listen, hand, fingers, nails, arma, and bilbow.

Alice
D'elbow, madame.

Elbow, madam.

Katharine
O Seigneur Dieu, je m'en oublie!
D'elbow.Comment appelez-vous le col?

Oh, I forgot! Elbow. What is the word for "le col?"

Alice
De nick, madame.

Neck, madam.

Katharine
De nick. Et le menton?

Nick. And "le menton?"

Alice
De chin.

Le menton is chin.

Katharine
De sin. Le col, de nick; le menton, de sin.

Neck and sin.

Alice
Oui. Sauf votre honneur, en verite, vous prononcez lesmots aussi droit que les natifs d'Angleterre.

Yes. Your Highness sounds just like a native speaker of English.

Katharine
Je ne doute point d'apprendre, par la grace de

I will learn it quickly, I think, God willing.

Dieu,et en peu de temps.

Alice
N'avez-vous pas deja oublie ce que je vous ai enseigne?

You remember what I just taught you?

Katharine
Non, je reciterai a vous promptement: d'hand, defingres, de mails,--

Let me see. Hand, fingers, nails...

Alice
De nails, madame.

Nails...

Katharine
De nails, de arm, de ilbow.

Nails, arm, ilbow.

Alice
Sauf votre honneur, de elbow.

Sorry, elbow.

Katharine
Ainsi dis-je; d'elbow, de nick, et de sin. Commentappelez-vous le pied et la robe?

That's what I said. Elbow, nick, and sin. What are the words for "le pied" and "la robe?"

Alice
De foot, madame; et de coun.

Foot, madam, and count.

Katharine
De foot et de coun! O Seigneur Dieu! ce sont mots de sonmauvais, corruptible, gros, et impudique, et non pour lesdames d'honneur d'user. Je ne voudrais prononcer ces motsdevant les seigneurs de France pour tout le monde. Foh! lefoot et le coun! Neanmoins, je reciterai une autre fois ma lecon ensemble: d' hand, de fingres, de nails, d'arm, d'elbow, de nick, de sin, de foot, de coun.

Foot and count! Those are ugly words, for a respectable girl to say. I would not say those words in front of the lords of France. Ugh! Foot and count! However, I will say them once more. Hand, fingers, nails, arm, elbow, nick, sin, foot, and coun.

Alice
Excellent, madame!

Excellent, madam.

Katharine
C'est assez pour une fois: allons-nous a diner.

That's enough for one day. Let's go eat.

Exit.

Scene V: The same.

Enter the King of France, the Dauphin, the duke of Bourbon, the Constable of France, and Others.

French King

'Tis certain he hath pass'd the river Somme.

It is true. He has passed the river Somme.

Constable

And if he be not fought withal, my lord,Let us not live in France; let us quit allAnd give our vineyards to a barbarous people.

If we don't fight back, let's not live in France and give all of our land to a barbarous people.

Dauphin

O Dieu vivant! shall a few sprays of us,The emptying of our fathers' luxury,Our scions put in wild and savage stock,Spirt up so suddenly into the clouds,And overlook their grafters?

My God! Are we forgetting what our fathers did?

Bourbon

Normans, but bastard Normans, Norman bastards!Mort de ma vie! if they march alongUnfought withal, but I will sell my dukedom,To buy a slobbery and a dirty farmIn that nook-shotten isle of Albion.

Normans! Norman bastards! If we don't fight back, I will sell my land for a filthy farm on the isle of Albion.

Constable

Dieu de batailles! where have they this mettle?Is not their climate foggy, raw, and dull,On whom, as in despite, the sun looks pale,Killing their fruit with frowns? Can sodden water,A drench for sur-rein'd jades, their barley-broth,Decoct their cold blood to such valiant heat?And shall our quick blood, spirited with wine,Seem frosty? O, for honour of our land,Let us not hang like roping iciclesUpon our houses' thatch, whiles a more frosty peopleSweat drops of gallant youth in our rich fields!Poor we may call them in their native lords.

God of battles! Where did they get their power? Is our blood so frosty, while theirs is running hot? Let's not hang around like icicles, while these cold brutes drop sweat upon our fields!

Dauphin

By faith and honour,Our madams mock at us, and plainly sayOur mettle is bred out, and they will giveTheir bodies to the lust of English youthTo new-store France with bastard warriors.

I swear our women make fun of us and say our courage is all gone, and they will give themselves to the English youth to breed new French warriors.

Bourbon

They bid us to the English dancing-schools,And teach lavoltas high, and swift corantos;Saying our grace is only in our heels,And that we are most lofty runaways.

They say the English are taking us to school and we are running away from their approach.

French King

Where is Montjoy the herald? Speed him hence.Let him greet England with our sharp defiance.Up, princes! and, with spirit of honour edgedMore sharper than your swords, hie to the field!Charles Delabreth, High Constable of France;You Dukes of Orleans, Bourbon, and of Berri,Alencon, Brabant, Bar, and Burgundy;Jacques Chatillon, Rambures, Vaudemont,Beaumont, Grandpre, Roussi, and Fauconberg,Foix, Lestrale, Bouciqualt, and Charolois;High dukes, great princes, barons, lords, and knights,For your great seats now quit you of great shames.Bar Harry England, that sweeps through our landWith pennons painted in the blood of Harfleur.Rush on his host, as doth the melted snowUpon the valleys, whose low vassal seatThe Alps doth spit and void his rheum upon.Go down upon him, you have power enough,And in a captive chariot into RouenBring him our prisoner.

Where is Montjoy, the herald? Bring him here quickly. Let him greet England with our sharp defiance. Get up, princes and go to the field. Charles Delabreth, high constable of France; you dukes of Orleans, Bourbon, and Berri, Alencon, Brabant, Bar, and Burgundy; Jaques Chatillon, Rambures, Vaudemont, Beaumont, Grandpre, Roussi, and Fauconberg; Foix, Lestrale, Bouciqualt, and Charolois show your bravery and fight Harry of England who sweeps through our land stained with the blood of Harfleur. Rush upon him like the snowy Alps and bring him back as our prisoner.

Constable

This becomes the great.Sorry am I his numbers are so few,His soldiers sick and famish'd in their march;For I am sure, when he shall see our army,He'll drop his heart into the sink of fearAnd for achievement offer us his ransom.

We will be great in number and he will be so few with his soldiers suffering with sickness and starvation. I am sure when he sees our army his heart will be filled with fear and he will give up.

French King

Therefore, Lord Constable, haste on Montjoy, And let him say to England that we sendTo know what willing ransom he will give.Prince Dauphin, you shall stay with us in Rouen.

Therefore, Lord Constable, hurry up Montjoy. Let him ask England what they will give us for the King's ransom. Prince Dauphin, you will stay with us here in Rouen.

Dauphin

Not so, I do beseech your Majesty.

No, please, your majesty.

French King

Be patient, for you shall remain with us.Now forth, Lord Constable and princes all,And quickly bring us word of England's fall.

Be patient. You will stay with us. Now, Lord Constable and princes, quickly bring us the news of England's downfall.

Exit.

Scene VI: the English camp in Picardy.

Enter Gower and Fluellen, meeting.

Gower
How now, Captain Fluellen! come you from the bridge?

How is it going, Captain Fluellen? Are you coming from the bridge?

Fluellen
I assure you, there is very excellent services committed at the bridge.

Yes, and I can assure you they are well committed at the bridge.

Gower
Is the Duke of Exeter safe?

Is the Duke of Exeter safe?

Fluellen
The Duke of Exeter is as magnanimous as Agamemnon; and aman that I love and honour with my soul, and my heart, and my duty, and my live, and my living, and my uttermost power. He is not--God be praised and blessed!-- any hurt in the world; but keeps the bridge most valiantly, with excellent discipline. There is an aunchient lieutenant there at the pridge, I think in my very conscience he is as valiant a man as Mark Antony; and he is a man of no estimation in the world, but I did see him do as gallant service.

The Duke of Exeter is well and unhurt. He keeps the bridge courageously and with excellent discipline. There is an old lieutenant at the bridge who is as brave as Mark Antony. He is a nobody, but he is performing a great service.

Gower
What do you call him?

What is his name?

Fluellen
He is call'd Aunchient Pistol.

He is called Pistol.

Gower
I know him not.

I don't know him.

Enter Pistol.

Fluellen
Here is the man.

Here he is.

Pistol
Captain, I thee beseech to do me favours.The Duke of Exeter doth love thee well.

Captain, I need to ask you for a favor. The Duke of Exeter loves you.

Fluellen

Ay, I praise God; and I have merited some love at his hands.

Praise God, I have earned his love.

Pistol

Bardolph, a soldier, firm and sound of heart,And of buxom valour, hath by cruel fateAnd giddy Fortune's furious fickle wheel,That goddess blind,That stands upon the rolling restless stone--

Bardolph, a good and valiant soldier, has encountered the cruel fate of blind Fortune's fickle wheel...

Fluellen

By your patience, Aunchient Pistol. Fortune is paintedblind, with a muffler afore his eyes, to signify to you that Fortune is blind; and she is painted also with a wheel, tosignify to you, which is the moral of it, that she is turning, and inconstant, and mutability, and variation; and her foot, look you, is fixed upon a spherical stone, which rolls, and rolls, and rolls. In good truth, the poet makes a most excellent description of it. Fortune is an excellent moral.

Pistol, Fortune is blind and holds a wheel of chance to show you the inconstancy of fate. She stands upon a rolling stone to show you the variability of luck. The poet who describes Fortune does an excellent job at explaining the moral.

Pistol

Fortune is Bardolph's foe, and frowns on him;For he hath stolen a pax, and hanged must 'a be,--A damned death!Let gallows gape for dog; let man go free,And let not hemp his windpipe suffocate.But Exeter hath given the doom of deathFor pax of little price.Therefore, go speak; the Duke will hear thy voice;And let not Bardolph's vital thread be cutWith edge of penny cord and vile reproach.
Speak, captain, for his life, and I will thee requite.

Fortune is Bardolph's foe and frowns on him. He stole a picture from church and must be hanged. A terrible death! A death for dogs. Let him go free and not suffocate on the end of a rope. Please, go talk to the duke. He will listen to you. Don't let Bardolph's life be ended this way. I will pay you back, if you will talk to him.

Fluellen

Aunchient Pistol, I do partly understand your meaning.

Lieutenant Pistol, I partly understand what you want.

Pistol

Why then, rejoice therefore.

Good.

Fluellen

Certainly, aunchient, it is not a thing to rejoice

Lieutenant, it's not good. Look, if he were my

at; for if, look you, he were my brother, I would desire the Duketo use his good pleasure, and put him to execution; fordiscipline ought to be used.

brother, I would want the duke to use his discretion and discipline him with execution, if necessary.

Pistol
Die and be damn'd! and figo for thy friendship!

Well, then die and go to hell! Forget our friendship!

Fluellen
It is well.

Oh, it's just as well.

Pistol
The fig of Spain.

Forget you!

Fluellen
Very good.

Exit.

Very good.

Gower
Why, this is an arrant counterfeit rascal. I rememberhim now; a bawd, a cutpurse.

Why, I remember that fellow. He is a fake rascal and a thief.

Fluellen
I'll assure you, 'a uttered as prave words at the pridge as you shall see in a summer's day. But it is very well; what he has spoke to me, that is well, I warrant you, when time is serve.

You should have heard him at the bridge, speaking as bravely as anyone. But it's all well. I promise you when the time is right.

Gower
Why, 't is a gull, a fool, a rogue, that now and then goes to the wars, to grace himself at his return into London under the form of a soldier. And such fellows are perfect in the great commanders' names; and they will learn you by rote where services were done; at such and such a sconce, at such a breach, at such a convoy; who came off bravely, who was shot, who disgrac'd, what terms the enemy stood on; and this they con perfectly in the phrase of war, which they trick up with new-tuned oaths: and what a beard of the general's cut and a horrid suit of the camp will do among foaming bottles and ale-wash'd wits, is wonderful to be thought on. But you must learn to know such slanders of the age, or else you may be marvellously

It is a fool, a rogue, who goes to wars now and then just to call himself a soldier. They can remember great commanders' names and talk about this breach or convoy or who was brave, or disgraced, or shot. They turn their experience into a means to trick others. You must beware of soldiers like these or be taken by them.

mistook.

Fluellen

I tell you what, Captain Gower; I do perceive he is not the man that he would gladly make show to the world he is. If I find a hole in his coat, I will tell him my mind. [Drum heard.] Hark you, the King is coming, and I must speak with him from the pridge.

God bless your Majesty!

King

How now, Fluellen! cam'st thou from the bridge?

Fluellen

Ay, so please your Majesty. The Duke of Exeter has verygallantly maintain'd the pridge. The French is gone off, look you; and there is gallant and most prave passages. Marry, th' athversary was have possession of the pridge; but he is enforced to retire, and the Duke of Exeter is master of the pridge. I can tell your Majesty, the Duke is a prave man.

King

What men have you lost, Fluellen?

Fluellen

The perdition of the athversary hath been very great, reasonable great. Marry, for my part, I think the Duke hath lost never a man, but one that is like to be executed for robbing a church, one Bardolph, if your Majesty know the man. His face is all bubukles, and whelks, and knobs, and flames o' fire; and his lips blows at his nose, and it is like a coal of fire, sometimes plue and sometimes red; but his nose is executed, and his fire's out.

I know, Captain Gower, he is not the man he'd like for people to think he is. And, given a chance, I will tell him what I think.

Drum heard.

Listen, the king is coming and I must speak with him from the bridge.

Drum and colors. Enter King Henry, Gloucester, and Soldiers.

God bless your majesty!

How are you, Fluellen? Are you coming from the bridge?

Yes, your majesty. The Duke of Exeter has maintained the bridge. The French are gone. The Duke is a master and he ran them off. He is a brave man.

What men have you lost, Fluellen?

The enemy lost many, but I don't think the duke lost a man, but one, who will be executed for robbing a church. His name is Bardolph, if you know him. His face is red and filled with whelps. He blows his nose making it red, but I guess he won't be blowing it anymore.

King

We would have all such offenders so cut off;
and we give express charge, that in our marches
through the country, there be nothing compell'd
from the villages, nothing taken but paid for,
none of the French upbraided or abused in
disdainful language; for when lenity and cruelty
play for a kingdom, the gentler gamester is the
soonest winner.

We want all such offenders cut off. No one is to take anything while we march, unless it is paid for. None of the French are to be abused or mistreated, because the gentlest player for a kingdom always wins.

A trumpet sounds. Montjoy enters.

Montjoy

You know me by my habit.

You can tell who I am.

King

Well then I know thee. What shall I know of thee?

Well, then I know you. What do you have to say?

Montjoy

My master's mind.

I'm here to speak my master's mind.

King

Unfold it.

Go ahead.

Montjoy

Thus says my King: Say thou to Harry of
England: Though we seem'd dead, we did but
sleep; advantage is a better soldier than
rashness. Tell him we could have rebuk'd him at
Harfleur, but that we thought not good to bruise
an injury till it were full ripe. Now we speak
upon our cue, and our voice is imperial. England
shall repent his folly, see his weakness, and
admire our sufferance. Bid him therefore
consider of his ransom; which must proportion
the losses we have borne, the subjects we have
lost, the disgrace we have digested; which in
weight to re-answer, his pettishness would bow
under. For our losses, his exchequer is too poor;
for the effusion of our blood, the muster of his
kingdom too faint a number; and for our
disgrace, his own person, kneeling at our feet,
but a weak and worthless satisfaction. To this
add defiance; and tell him, for conclusion, he
hath betrayed his followers, whose

My king says to tell you though we seem dead, we were just asleep. We could have rebuked you at Harfleur, but we were waiting until the perfect time. England must turn back, admit his weakness, and we will be merciful. Therefore, think about what you are asking and the losses we have already taken in addition to the disgrace we have digested, which is far weightier than yours. You can do nothing to make amends for your actions. You have betrayed your men who will be condemned.

condemnation is pronounc'd. So far my King and master; so much my office.

King
What is thy name? I know thy quality.

What is your name? You seem familiar.

Montjoy
Montjoy.

Montjoy

King
Thou dost thy office fairly. Turn thee back,And tell thy King I do not seek him now,But could be willing to march on to Calais Without impeachment; for, to say the sooth,Though 'tis no wisdom to confess so muchUnto an enemy of craft and vantage,My people are with sickness much enfeebled,My numbers lessen'd, and those few I haveAlmost no better than so many French;Who when they were in health, I tell thee, herald,I thought upon one pair of English legsDid march three Frenchmen. Yet, forgive me, God,That I do brag thus! This your air of FranceHath blown that vice in me. I must repent.Go therefore, tell thy master here I am;My ransom is this frail and worthless trunk,My army but a weak and sickly guard;Yet, God before, tell him we will come on,Though France himself and such another neighbourStand in our way. There's for thy labour, Montjoy.Go, bid thy master well advise himself.If we may pass, we will; if we be hind'red,We shall your tawny ground with your red bloodDiscolour; and so, Montjoy, fare you well.The sum of all our answer is but this:We would not seek a battle, as we are;Nor, as we are, we say we will not shun it.So tell your master.

You do a good job. Now, go back and tell the king I am not seeking him now. But I could be persuaded to march on to Calais, if he would like. However, I shouldn't admit my intentions. My people are sick and weak. The number of my soldiers is down and those I have, whom I thought were worth three Frenchmen, are not well. Let me not brag, God. Go tell your master I am ready to repent, and even though my desires are worthless and my army is weak, we are coming. This is for your trouble, Montjoy. Go tell your master if he resists us, we will paint the ground blood red. Tell your master we do not seek a battle, but we will not avoid one.

Montjoy
I shall deliver so. Thanks to your Highness.

I will deliver your message. Thanks, your highness.

Gloucester

Exit.

I hope they will not come upon us now.

I hope they don't attack us now.

King

We are in God's hands, brother, not in theirs.March to the bridge; it now draws toward night.Beyond the river we'll encamp ourselves,And on to-morrow bid them march away.

We are in God's hands, not the French. It's almost night time, so march to the bridge. We will camp beyond the river and tomorrow, we will march.

Exit.

Scene VII: The French camp, near Agincourt.

Enter the Constable of France, the Lord Rambures, Orleans, and Dauphin with others.

Constable
Tut! I have the best armour of the world. Would it were day!

Bull! I have the best armor in the world. I wish it were day!

Orleans
You have an excellent armour; but let my horse have his due.

You do have an excellent armor, but don't forget about my horses.

Constable
It is the best horse of Europe.

You do have the best horse in Europe.

Orleans
Will it never be morning?

Will it never be morning?

Dauphin
My Lord of Orleans, and my Lord High Constable, you talk of horse and armour?

My lord of Orleans and my lord high Constable, are you talking of horses and armor?

Orleans
You are as well provided of both as any prince in the world.

Yes, and you have the best of both as any prince in the world.

Dauphin
What a long night is this! I will not change my horse withany that treads but on four pasterns. Ca, ha! he bounds from the earth, as if his entrails were hairs; le cheval volant, the Pegasus, chez les narines de feu! When I bestride him, I soar, I am a hawk. he trots the air; the earth sings when he touches it; the basest horn of his hoof is more musical than the pipe of Hermes.

What a long night this is! I would not trade my horse for another. He bounds from the earth like Pegasus. I feel like I am flying when I sit on him. The earth sings at the touch of his hoof which is as musical as the pipe of Hermes.

Orleans
He's of the colour of the nutmeg.

He's the color of nutmeg.

Dauphin
And of the heat of the ginger. It is a beast for Perseus. He is pure air and fire; and the dull elements of earth and water never appear in him, but only in patient stillness while his rider

And he has the heat of ginger. He is a beast fit for Perseus, pure air and fire. He is only calm when he is mounted by his rider. All other horses pale in comparison.

mounts him. He is indeed a horse, and all other jades you may call beasts.

Constable
Indeed, my lord, it is a most absolute and excellent horse.

Indeed, my lord, he is an excellent horse.

Dauphin
It is the prince of palfreys; his neigh is like the bidding of a monarch, and his countenance enforces homage.

He is the prince of horses. His neigh is like the bidding of a king and he demands honor.

Orleans
No more, cousin.

No more, cousin.

Dauphin
Nay, the man hath no wit that cannot, from the rising of the lark to the lodging of the lamb, vary deserved praise on my palfrey. It is a theme as fluent as the sea; turn the sands into eloquent tongues, and my horse is argument for them all. 'Tis a subject for a sovereign to reason on, and for a sovereign's sovereign to ride on; and for the world, familiar to us and unknown, to lay apart their particular functions and wonder at him. I once writ a sonnet in his praise and began thus: "Wonder of nature,"--

No, the man has no sense if he can't praise my horse. He is as worthy a subject for a king. I even wrote a sonnet based on him: "Wonder of nature..."

Orleans
I have heard a sonnet begin so to one's mistress.

I heard a sonnet about one's mistress that started the same way.

Dauphin
Then did they imitate that which I compos'd to my courser,for my horse is my mistress.

Then, they must have copied mine, because my horse is my mistress.

Orleans
Your mistress bears well.

Your mistress serves you well.

Dauphin
Me well; which is the prescript praise and perfection of agood and particular mistress.

Exactly why I call her my mistress.

Constable
Nay, for methought yesterday your mistress shrewdly shookyour back.

That's not what I saw yesterday when she threw you off her back.

Dauphin

So perhaps did yours.

Maybe yours did.

Constable

Mine was not bridled.

Mine wasn't bridled.

Dauphin

O then belike she was old and gentle; and you rode, like akern of Ireland, your French hose off, and in your straitstrossers.

Perhaps she is too old and gentle, so you rode like an Irishman, without pants.

Constable

You have good judgment in horsemanship.

You are a good judge of horsemanship.

Dauphin

Be warn'd by me, then; they that ride so and ride not warily, fall into foul bogs. I had rather have my horse to my mistress.

Well, let me warn you. He that rides like that falls into trouble. I'd rather have my horse than my mistress.

Constable

I had as lief have my mistress a jade.

I'll keep my mistress.

Dauphin

I tell thee, Constable, my mistress wears his own hair.

I tell you, Constable, at least my mistress has her own hair.

Constable

I could make as true a boast as that, if I had a sow tomy mistress.

I could make the same boast, if my mistress was a pig.

Dauphin

"Le chien est retourne a son propre vomissement, et latruie lavee au bourbier." Thou mak'st use of anything.

"The dog returns to his own vomit and the pig to its mud." You would make anything your mistress.

Constable

Yet do I not use my horse for my mistress, or any suchproverb so little kin to the purpose.

Yet, I don't use my horse for my mistress or any other think like it.

Rambures

My Lord Constable, the armour that I saw in your tentto-night, are those stars or suns upon it?

My lord Constable, are there stars or suns on the armor I saw in your tent tonight?

Constable

Stars, my lord.

Stars, my lord.

Dauphin
Some of them will fall to-morrow, I hope.

I hope some of them will fall tomorrow.

Constable
And yet my sky shall not want.

But, my sky will not be left in want.

Dauphin
That may be, for you bear a many superfluously, and 'tweremore honour some were away.

You wear too many, anyway.

Constable
Even as your horse bears your praises; who would trot aswell, were some of your brags dismounted.

Not as many as the praises you heap upon your horse.

Dauphin
Would I were able to load him with his desert! Will it never be day? I will trot to-morrow a mile, and my way shall bepaved with English faces.

I still can't give him enough praises. Will it ever be day? I will ride a mile tomorrow and pave the way with Englishmen.

Constable
I will not say so, for fear I should be fac'd out of my way. But I would it were morning; for I would fain be aboutthe ears of the English.

I wouldn't say that. You shouldn't brag, but I do wish it was morning, because I am ready to face the English.

Rambures
Who will go to hazard with me for twenty prisoners?

Would anyone like to bet me twenty prisoners?

Constable
You must first go yourself to hazard, ere you have them.

You have to get them, first.

Dauphin
'Tis midnight; I'll go arm myself.

It's midnight. I'm going to get prepared.

Exit.

Orleans
The Dauphin longs for morning.

The Dauphin can't wait until morning.

Rambures
He longs to eat the English.

He's ready to eat the English.

70

Constable
I think he will eat all he kills.

I think he will be able to eat all he kills.

Orleans
By the white hand of my lady, he's a gallant prince.

I swear by the white hand of my lady, he is a brave prince.

Constable
Swear by her foot that she may tread out the oath.

You'd be better off to swear by her foot.

Orleans
He is simply the most active gentleman of France.

He is the most active gentleman in France.

Constable
Doing is activity; and he will still be doing.

Acting is activity, and he's always doing that.

Orleans
He never did harm, that I heard of.

He never has harmed anyone that I know of.

Constable
Nor will do none to-morrow. He will keep that goodname still.

Nor will he tomorrow. He will keep his good name, still.

Orleans
I know him to be valiant.

I think he is courageous.

Constable
I was told that by one that knows him better than you.

Someone who knows him better than you told me that.

Orleans
What's he?

Who?

Constable
Marry, he told me so himself; and he said he car'd notwho knew it.

He told me so himself, and he said he didn't care who knew it.

Orleans
He needs not; it is no hidden virtue in him.

Well, he doesn't have to be brave. It's not a hard virtue to see.

Constable
By my faith, sir, but it is; never anybody saw it but hislackey. 'Tis a hooded valour; and when

I swear, sir, valor is never easy to see. No one has ever seen him be brave, but his servant, and it appears, it willbate.

then it was short-lived.

Orleans
"Ill will never said well."

You shouldn't speak ill of him.

Constable
I will cap that proverb with "There is flattery in friendship."

And, flattery is found among friends.

Orleans
And I will take up that with "Give the devil his due."

Just, giving the devil his due.

Constable
Well plac'd. There stands your friend for the devil; have at the very eye of that proverb with "A pox of the devil."

That's a good word for him, the devil.

Orleans
You are the better at proverbs, by how much "A fool'sbolt is soon shot."

You are better at using proverbs for a fool shoots quickly and often misses his mark.

Constable
You have shot over.

You have over shot your friend.

Orleans
'Tis not the first time you were overshot.

It's not the first time.

Enter a messenger.

Messenger
My Lord High Constable, the English lie within fifteenhundred paces of your tents.

My lord, high Constable, the English are within fifteen hundred feet from your tents.

Constable
Who hath measur'd the ground?

Who measured the ground?

Messenger
The Lord Grandpre.

The Lord Grandpre.

Constable
A valiant and most expert gentleman. Would it were day!Alas, poor Harry of England, he longs not for the dawning as we do.

Now, that's a valiant gentleman. I wish it were day! I bet poor Harry of England doesn't though.

Orleans

What a wretched and peevish fellow is this King of England, to mope with his fat-brain'd followers so far out of his knowledge!

He is a wretched and stupid fellow to bring his fat-headed followers to France, where he doesn't know anything.

Constable
If the English had any apprehension, they would run away.

If the English had any sense, they'd run away.

Orleans
That they lack; for if their heads had any intellectual armour, they could never wear such heavy head-pieces.

They don't have any brains in their heads or else they couldn't wear such heavy armor.

Rambures
That island of England breeds very valiant creatures. Their mastiffs are of unmatchable courage.

The island of England breeds very valiant creatures; their dogs are of unmatchable courage.

Orleans
Foolish curs, that run winking into the mouth of a Russian bear and have their heads crush'd like rotten apples! You may as well say, that's a valiant flea that dare eat his breakfast on the lip of a lion.

They're foolish dogs to run blind into the mouth of a bear that will crush their heads like apples! You might as well say they are valiant fleas eating their breakfast on the lip of a lion.

Constable
Just, just; and the men do sympathize with the mastiffs in robustious and rough coming on, leaving their wits with their wives; and then, give them great meals of beef and iron and steel, they will eat like wolves and fight like devils.

We men must feel sorry for these dogs that left their brains behind with their wives. Then they are given them meals of beef and iron to eat like wolves and fight like devils.

Orleans
Ay, but these English are shrewdly out of beef.

Yes, but these English are out of beef.

Constable
Then shall we find to-morrow they have only stomachs to eat and none to fight. Now is it time to arm. Come, shall we about it?

Then I hope we find tomorrow they don't have the stomachs to fight. Now, it's time to prepare. Shall we go?

Orleans
It is now two o'clock; but, let me see, by ten We shall have each a hundred Englishmen.

It's only two o'clock, but let me see, by ten tomorrow, we will each have a hundred Englishmen.

Exit.

Act IV

Prologue

Enter Chorus.

Now entertain conjecture of a timeWhen creeping murmur and the poring darkFills the wide vessel of the universe.From camp to camp through the foul womb of nightThe hum of either army stilly sounds,That the fix'd sentinels almost receiveThe secret whispers of each other's watch;Fire answers fire, and through their paly flamesEach battle sees the other's umber'd face;Steed threatens steed, in high and boastful neighsPiercing the night's dull ear; and from the tentsThe armourers, accomplishing the knights,With busy hammers closing rivets up,Give dreadful note of preparation.The country cocks do crow, the clocks do toll,And the third hour of drowsy morning name.Proud of their numbers and secure in soul,The confident and over-lusty FrenchDo the low-rated English play at dice;And chide the cripple tardy-gaited NightWho, like a foul and ugly witch, doth limpSo tediously away. The poor condemned English,Like sacrifices, by their watchful firesSit patiently and inly ruminateThe morning's danger; and their gesture sad,Investing lank-lean cheeks and war-worn coats,Presented them unto the gazing moonSo many horrid ghosts. O now, who will beholdThe royal captain of this ruin'd bandWalking from watch to watch, from tent to tent,Let him cry, "Praise and glory on his head!"For forth he goes and visits all his host,Bids them good morrow with a modest smile,And calls them brothers, friends, and countrymen.Upon his royal face there is no noteHow dread an army hath enrounded him;Nor doth he dedicate one jot of colourUnto the weary and all-watched night,But freshly looks, and over-bears attaintWith cheerful semblance and sweet

Now entertain a brief passing of time when night surrounds the earth. From camp to camp, hear the hum of army sounds and the secret whispers of each sentinel's watch. Men answer fire with fire, staring into the other's face. Horses threaten other horses with high-pitched neighs, piercing the soundless night. From tents, you hear the men being placed in their armor. Take note of the dreadful preparation for war. The country cocks crow and the clocks toll the third hour of morning. The proud and over-lusty French, secure in their numbers, go to meet the English as night passes, like an ugly limping witch. The poor condemned English wait like sacrifices by their fire and think about the morning's danger. Their faces are sad and lean, and their coats are worn from war. Behold the royal captain going from tent to tent crying, "Praise and glory be!" He bids them good morning with a modest smile and calls them brothers, friends, and countrymen. He appears unaware of the condition of his men, but looks fresh and cheerful so every man may take comfort from him. He looks upon each man, cold with fear, and gives them a piece of himself. Now, our scene takes us to battle at Agincourt. Watch our performance and remember our story.

majesty;That every wretch, pining and pale before,Beholding him, plucks comfort from his looks.A largess universal like the sunHis liberal eye doth give to every one,Thawing cold fear, that mean and gentle allBehold, as may unworthiness define,A little touch of Harry in the night.And so our scene must to the battle fly,Where--O for pity!--we shall much disgraceWith four or five most vile and ragged foils,Right ill-dispos'd in brawl ridiculous,The name of Agincourt. Yet sit and see,Minding true things by what their mock'ries be.

Exit.

Scene I: The English camp at Agincourt.

Enter King Henry, Bedford, and Gloucester.

King
Gloucester, 'tis true that we are in great danger;The greater therefore should our courage be.Good morrow, brother Bedford. God Almighty!There is some soul of goodness in things evil,Would men observingly distil it out;For our bad neighbour makes us early stirrers,Which is both healthful and good husbandry.Besides, they are our outward consciences,And preachers to us all, admonishingThat we should dress us fairly for our end.Thus may we gather honey from the weed,And make a moral of the devil himself.

Gloucester, it's true we are in great danger, so we must be more courageous. Good morning, brother Bedford. God almighty, there are still some good found among evil. Our bad neighbor makes us early risers, which is both healthy and noble. Besides, they are like preachers to us, reprimanding us so we should be ready for the end, so we may take the good from the bad and find the moral of all this.

Enter Erpingham.

Good morrow, old Sir Thomas Erpingham:A good soft pillow for that good white headWere better than a churlish turf of France.

Good morning, old Sir Thomas Erpingham. I bet you wish you had a soft pillow for that white head than the hard ground of France.

Erpingham
Not so, my liege; this lodging likes me better,Since I may say, "Now lie I like a king."

Not so, my king, this lodging is just fine by me, since I can say, "Now I lay just like a king."

King
'Tis good for men to love their present painsUpon example; so the spirit is eased;And when the mind is quick'ned, out of doubt,The organs, though defunct and dead before,Break up their drowsy grave and newly move,With casted slough and fresh legerity.Lend me thy cloak, Sir Thomas. Brothers both,Commend me to the princes in our camp;Do my good morrow to them, and anonDesire them all to my pavilion.

It's good for men to embrace their present pains to ease their spirits when their minds are filled with doubt. It awakens the body and gives a fresh perspective on life. Lend me your cloak, Sir Thomas. Both of you, give my pardons to the princes in our camp and tell them good morning. Tell them they are welcome in my tent, if they would like.

Gloucester
We shall, my liege.

We will, my liege.

Erpingham
Shall I attend your Grace?

Should I go, your grace?

King

No, my good knight;Go with my brothers to my lords of England.I and my bosom must debate a while,And then I would no other company.

Erpingham

The Lord in heaven bless thee, noble Harry!

King

God-a-mercy, old heart! thou speak'st cheerfully.

Pistol

Qui va la?

King

A friend.

Pistol

Discuss unto me; art thou officer?Or art thou base, common, and popular?

King

I am a gentleman of a company.

Pistol

Trail'st thou the puissant pike?

King

Even so. What are you?

Pistol

As good a gentleman as the Emperor.

King

Then you are a better than the King.

Pistol

The King's a bawcock, and a heart of gold,A lad of life, an imp of fame;Of parents good, of fist most valiant.I kiss his dirty shoe, and from heart-stringI love the lovely bully. What is thy name?

No, my good knight, go with my brothers to my lords of England. We must talk awhile and then I want to be alone.

May the Lord in heaven bless you, noble Harry!

Exit all but King Henry.

God have mercy, old heart! You speak cheerfully.

Enter Pistol.

Who are you?

A friend.

Are you an officer or are you a common man?

I am a gentleman of one of the companies.

Do you carry a pike?

Yes. What are you?

I am a gentleman as good as the emperor.

Then you are better than the king.

The king is a great man with a heart of gold. He is all about life, not fame. He comes from good parents and is most valiant. I would kiss his dirty shoe. I love him. What is your name?

King
Harry le Roy.

Harry LeRoy.

Pistol
Le Roy! a Cornish name. Art thou of Cornish crew?

That's a Cornish name. Are you Cornish?

King
No, I am a Welshman.

No, I am a Welshman.

Pistol
Know'st thou Fluellen?

Do you know Fluellen?

King
Yes.

Yes.

Pistol
Tell him I'll knock his leek about his pateUpon Saint Davy's day.

Then, tell him, I'm going to knock his block off on St. Davy's day.

King
Do not you wear your dagger in your cap that day, lesthe knock that about yours.

You better not wear your dagger in your hat or he might knock yours off.

Pistol
Art thou his friend?

Are you his friend?

King
And his kinsman too.

And his relative, too.

Pistol
The figo for thee, then!

To hell with you, then!

King
I thank you. God be with you!

Thanks. God be with you!

Pistol
My name is Pistol call'd.

My name is Pistol.

Exit.

King
It sorts well with your fierceness.

The name suits your fierceness.

Enter Fluellen and Gower.

Gower

Captain Fluellen!

Fluellen
So! in the name of Jesu Christ, speak lower. It is the greatest admiration in the universal world, when the true and aunchient prerogatifes and laws of the wars is not kept. If you would take the pains but to examine the wars of Pompey the Great, youshall find, I warrant you, that there is no tiddle taddle nor pibble pabble in Pompey's camp. I warrant you, you shall find the ceremonies of the wars, and the cares of it, and the forms of it, and the sobriety of it, and the modesty of it, to be otherwise.

Captain Fluellen!

In the name of Jesus, speak lower. It's a shame when people aren't aware of the laws of war. It would do you some good to examine the wars of Pompey, the Great. You will surely find no silliness in his camp, only the ceremonies and seriousness of war.

Gower
Why, the enemy is loud; you hear him all night.

Why? The enemy is loud. You hear them all night.

Fluellen
If the enemy is an ass and a fool and a prating coxcomb, is it meet, think you, that we should also, look you, be an ass and a fool and a prating coxcomb? In your own conscience, now?

Should we be fools, if the enemy is? Think about it.

Gower
I will speak lower.

I will be quieter.

Fluellen
I pray you and beseech you that you will.

I hope so.

Exit Gower and Fluellen.

King
Though it appear a little out of fashion,There is much care and valour in this Welshman.

It may not be popular, but there is much care in this Welshman.

Enter three soldiers, John Bates, Alexander Court, and Michael Williams.

Court
Brother John Bates, is not that the morning which breaksyonder?

Brother John Bates, isn't that the morning breaking over there?

Bates
I think it be; but we have no great cause to desire theapproach of day.

I think it is, but we are in no hurry for it.

Williams

We see yonder the beginning of the day, but I thinkwe shall never see the end of it. Who goes there?

King
A friend.

Williams
Under what captain serve you?

King
Under Sir Thomas Erpingham.

Williams
A good old commander and a most kind gentleman. Ipray you, what thinks he of our estate?

King
Even as men wreck'd upon a sand, that look to bewash'd off the next tide.

Bates
He hath not told his thought to the King?

King
No; nor it is not meet he should. For though I speak it to you, I think the King is but a man as I am. The violet smells to him as it doth to me; the element shows to him as it doth to me; all his senses have but human conditions. His ceremonies laid by, in his nakedness he appears but a man; and though his affections are higher mounted than ours, yet, when they stoop, they stoop with the like wing. Therefore, when he sees reason of fears as we do, his fears, out of doubt, be of the same relish as ours are; yet, in reason, no man should possess him with any appearance of fear, lest he, by showing it, should dishearten his army.

Bates
He may show what outward courage he will; but I believe, as cold a night as 'tis, he could wish himself in Thames up to the neck; and so I

We see the beginning of a new day, but I don't think we will see the end. Who goes there?

A friend.

What captain do you serve?

I serve under Sir Thomas Erpingham.

He is a good old commander and kind gentleman. May I ask, what he thinks of our situation?

He thinks we look like men wrecked on a beach about to be swept out to sea.

Has he told the king?

No, and I don't think he should. Even though I am telling you, the king is a man and can see the situation. He feels just like a man, and he fears just like a man, but he can't show it like a man or else his men would sense it and become disheartened.

He may appear courageous, but I bet he wishes he were in the Thames up to his neck. I know I would if I were him, I am so ready to be done

would he were, and I by him, at all adventures, so we were quit here.

King
By my troth, I will speak my conscience of the King: I think he would not wish himself anywhere but where he is.

Bates
Then I would he were here alone; so should he be sure to be ransomed, and a many poor men's lives saved.

King
I dare say you love him not so ill, to wish him here alone, howsoever you speak this to feel other men's minds. Methinks I could not die anywhere so contented as in the King's company, his cause being just and his quarrel honourable.

Williams
That's more than we know.

Bates
Ay, or more than we should seek after; for we know enough, if we know we are the King's subjects. If his cause be wrong, our obedience to the King wipes the crime of it out of us.

Williams
But if the cause be not good, the King himself hath a heavy reckoning to make, when all those legs and arms and heads, chopp'd off in a battle, shall join together at the latter day and cry all, "We died at such a place"; some swearing, some crying for a surgeon, some upon their wives left poor behind them, some upon the debts they owe, some upon their children rawly left. I am afeard there are few die well that die in a battle; for how can they charitably dispose of anything, when blood is their argument? Now, if these men do not die well, it will be a black matter for the King that led them to it; who to disobey were against all proportion of subjection.

here.

Honestly, I don't think he would rather be anywhere but here.

Then, I wish he were here alone for he would surely be ransomed and many men's lives would be spared.

I guess you don't love him so much, if you wish he were here alone, unless you are saying that just to feel out other men. I could not die anywhere as happily as with the king. His cause is just and his argument is honorable.

You know more than us.

Yes, or you know more than we should. Regardless of the valor in his argument, we are his subjects and must follow him.

If his cause is not good, he has a heavy reckoning to make, when all the legs, arms, and heads, chopped off in battle, join together on Judgment Day and cry, "We died at France." There are a few who will die well in battle, but how can a person expect forgiveness when they spent their lives killing? If these men go without God's grace, the king will have a heavy price to pay, because who of his subjects could refuse him.

King

So, if a son that is by his father sent about merchandise do sinfully miscarry upon the sea, the imputation of his wickedness, by your rule, should be imposed upon his father that sent him; or if a servant, under his master's command transporting a sum of money, be assailed by robbers and die in many irreconcil'diniquities, you may call the business of the master the author of the servant's damnation. But this is not so. The King is not bound to answer the particular endings of his soldiers, the father of his son, nor the master of his servant; for they purpose not their death, when they purpose their services. Besides, there is no king, be his cause never so spotless, if it come to thearbitrement of swords, can try it out with all unspotted soldiers. Some peradventure have on them the guilt of premeditated and contrived murder; some, of beguiling virgins with the broken seals of perjury; some, making the wars their bulwark, that have before gored the gentle bosom of Peace with pillage and robbery. Now, if these men have defeated the law and outrun native punishment, though they can outstrip men, they have no wings to fly from God. War is his beadle, war is his vengeance; so that here men are punish'd for before-breach of the King's laws in now the King's quarrel. Where they feared the death, they have borne life away; and where they would be safe, they perish. Then if they die unprovided, no more is the King guilty of their damnation than he was before guilty of those impieties for the which they are now visited. Every subject's duty is the King's; but every subject's soul is his own. Therefore should every soldier in the wars do as every sick man in his bed, wash every mote out of his conscience; and dying so, death is to him advantage; or not dying, the time was blessedly lost wherein such preparation was gained; and in him that escapes, it were not sin to think that, making God so free an offer, He let him outlive that day to see His greatness and to teach others how they should prepare.

So, if a son, dutiful to his father, is sent to commit sins upon the sea, the punishment should be on his father's head, or if a servant, under his master's command, gets robbed and killed, then it is the master's fault that sent him. It is not the fault of the father, the master or the king, because the others offer their deaths when they offer their services. Anyway, has there ever been a king whose men were blameless? Some may have been guilty of murder while others of stealing. If these men escaped prosecution at home, they cannot escape God's. War is a holy instrument of justice. So, some men pay for their crimes with their lives in the king's war. The king is no guiltier of their damnation as he was their earlier crimes. Every man is responsible for his own soul. Therefore, every man should make amends for their sins so in death they will have a clear conscience. And, if he doesn't die, he can live to tell his story to the glory of God.

Williams

'Tis certain, every man that dies ill, the ill upon his own head, the King is not to answer for it.

It's certain that any man who dies from illness, the illness is the fault of the king.

Bates

I do not desire he should answer for me; and yet I determine to fight lustily for him.

I don't want him to answer for me, and I willingly will fight for him.

King

I myself heard the King say he would not be ransom'd.

I heard the king say he would not be ransomed.

Williams

Ay, he said so, to make us fight cheerfully; but when ourthroats are cut, he may be ransom'd, and we ne'er the wiser.

He said that to make us fight harder, but when our throats are cut, he may be ransomed and we won't know the difference.

King

If I live to see it, I will never trust his word after.

If I live to see it, I won't believe him ever again.

Williams

You pay him then. That's a perilous shot out of an elder-gun, that a poor and a private displeasure can do against a monarch! You may as well go about to turn the sun to ice with fanning in his face with a peacock's feather. You'll never trust his word after! Come, 'tis a foolish saying.

You go tell him, then. What a pathetic threat! You may as well try to turn the sun to ice. "You'll never trust his word again." What a stupid thing to say.

King

Your reproof is something too round. I should be angry with you, if the time were convenient.

You are out of line. I would be angry if I had the time.

Williams

Let it be a quarrel between us if you live.

Well, if we live, let it be a quarrel between us.

King

I embrace it.

I will.

Williams

How shall I know thee again?

How will I know you again?

King

Give me any gage of thine, and I will wear it in my bonnet; then, if ever thou dar'st acknowledge it, I will make it my quarrel.

Give me something to remember you by and I will wear it in my bonnet. Then, if you acknowledge it, I will quarrel with you.

Williams

Here's my glove; give me another of thine.

Here's my glove. Give me one of yours.

King

There.

There.

Williams

This will I also wear in my cap. If ever thou come to meand say, after to-morrow, "This is my glove," by this hand I will take thee a box on the ear.

I will wear it in my cap, and if you ever come to me and say, "This is my glove," I will box you on the ear with this hand.

King

If ever I live to see it, I will challenge it.

If I live to see it, I will challenge you.

Williams

Thou dar'st as well be hang'd.

You might as well be hanged.

King

Well, I will do it, though I take thee in the King's company.

I will do it, even in front of the king.

Williams

Keep thy word; fare thee well.

Keep your word. Goodbye.

Bates

Be friends, you English fools, be friends. We haveFrench quarrels enow, if you could tell how to reckon.

Be friends, you English fools. We have enough French quarrels for you to worry about.

King

Indeed, the French may lay twenty French crowns to onethey will beat us, for they bear them on their shoulders; but it is no English treason to cut French crowns, and to-morrow the King himself will be a clipper.Upon the King! Let us our lives, our souls,Our debts, our careful wives,Our children, and our sins lay on the King!We must bear all. O hard condition,Twin-born with greatness, subject to the breathOf every fool, whose sense no more can feelBut his own wringing! What infinite heart's-easeMust kings neglect, that private men enjoy!And what have kings, that privates have not too,Save ceremony, save general

Indeed, the French may bet twenty one they will beat us, but we will cut them down alongside the king tomorrow.

Exit soldiers.

I swear, let us lay our lives, our souls, our debts, our wives, our children, and our sins on the king! I must bear it all. What a hard life to live, born with greatness and subject to every fool. What a king must bear, that a private man enjoys! What's the difference between a king and a common man. Just general ceremony? What kind of god suffers more than mortals?

ceremony?And what art thou, thou idol Ceremony?What kind of god art thou, that suffer'st moreOf mortal griefs than do thy worshippers?What are thy rents? What are thy comings in?O Ceremony, show me but thy worth!What is thy soul of adoration?Art thou aught else but place, degree, and form,Creating awe and fear in other men?Wherein thou art less happy being fear'dThan they in fearing.What drink'st thou oft, instead of homage sweet,But poison'd flattery? O, be sick, great greatness,And bid thy Ceremony give thee cure!Think'st thou the fiery fever will go outWith titles blown from adulation?Will it give place to flexure and low bending?Canst thou, when thou command'st the beggar's knee,Command the health of it? No, thou proud dream,That play'st so subtly with a king's repose;I am a king that find thee, and I know'Tis not the balm, the sceptre, and the ball,The sword, the mace, the crown imperial,The intertissued robe of gold and pearl,The farced title running 'fore the King,The throne he sits on, nor the tide of pompThat beats upon the high shore of this world,No, not all these, thrice-gorgeous Ceremony,--Not all these, laid in bed majestical,Can sleep so soundly as the wretched slave,Who with a body fill'd and vacant mindGets him to rest, cramm'd with distressful bread,Never sees horrid night, the child of hell,But, like a lackey, from the rise to setSweats in the eye of Phoebus, and all nightSleeps in Elysium; next day after dawn,Doth rise and help Hyperion to his horse,And follows so the ever-running year,With profitable labour, to his grave:And, but for ceremony, such a wretch,Winding up days with toil and nights with sleep,Had the fore-hand and vantage of a king.The slave, a member of the country's peace,Enjoys it, but in gross brain little wotsWhat watch the King keeps to maintain the peace,Whose hours the peasant best advantages.

What is the payment? What's it all worth? What makes a soul more worthy of adoration? Place and position in life to create fear in other men, while you are more unhappy being feared than the ones who are actually fearful? What good is useless flattery instead of sincere love? I am sick of all the ceremony. Give me a cure! Do you think a title gives so much credit men are eager to bend their knee? It's all a vain dream. I understand you, ceremony. I am a king, and I know nothing will help the king sleep like the common man, with an empty mind and full belly rests peacefully. He never wakes in the night, tormented like a child of hell. After years of labor he goes to his grave and rests in peace. He is better off than a king. He enjoys peace in his country without worrying about how to maintain it.

Erpingham

My lord, your nobles, jealous of your absence,Seek through your camp to find you.

King

Good old knight,Collect them all together at my tent.I'll be before thee.

Erpingham

I shall do't, my lord.

King

O God of battles! steel my soldiers' hearts.Possess them not with fear. Take from them nowThe sense of reckoning, if the opposed numbersPluck their hearts from them. Not to-day, O Lord,O, not to-day, think not upon the faultMy father made in compassing the crown!I Richard's body have interred new,And on it have bestow'd more contrite tearsThan from it issued forced drops of blood.Five hundred poor I have in yearly pay,Who twice a day their wither'd hands hold upToward heaven, to pardon blood; and I have builtTwo chantries, where the sad and solemn priestsSing still for Richard's soul. More will I do;Though all that I can do is nothing worth,Since that my penitence comes after all,Imploring pardon.

Gloucester

My liege!

King

My brother Gloucester's voice? Ay;I know thy errand, I will go with thee.The day, my friends, and all things stay for me.

Enter Erpingham

My lord, your nobles are looking for you throughout the camp.

Good old knight, get them all together at my tent. I'll be right there.

I'll do it, my lord.

Exit.

Oh God of battles! Make my soldiers' hearts steel. Take away their fear and their sense of revenge, if the enemy is too great. Oh Lord, don't think about the way my father took the crown today. Oh not today! I have cried more tears over Richard's body than he drew from this world. I employ five hundred people to pray for my absolution twice a day, and I've built two churches to house priests who sing continually for Richard's soul. I will do more, but nothing is worth your pardon.

Enter Gloucester

My liege!

Is that you, Gloucester? Yes, I know why you're here. I will go with you. Today, my friends and everything wait upon me.

Exit.

Scene II: The French camp.

Enter the Dauphin, Orleans, Rambures, and others.

Orleans
The sun doth gild our armour; up, my lords!

The sun is shining upon our armor. Get up, my lords!

Dauphin
Montez a cheval! My horse, varlet! lackey! ha!

Get on your horse. Get my horse! Ha!

Orleans
O brave spirit!

Oh, brave spirit!

Dauphin
Via! les eaux et la terre.

I will ride him through floods and fields.

Orleans
Rien puis? L'air et le feu.

What about through air and fire?

Dauphin
Ciel, cousin Orleans.

Just the heavens, cousin Orleans.

Enter Constable.

Now, my Lord Constable!

Hello, my lord, Constable!

Constable
Hark, how our steeds for present service neigh!

Hey, are our horses ready to serve us?

Dauphin
Mount them, and make incision in their hides,That their hot blood may spin in English eyes,And dout them with superfluous courage, ha!

When you mount them, cut them in their hides so the blood may spin out into the eyes of the English. Give them any extra courage you have, ha!

Rambures
What, will you have them weep our horses' blood?How shall we, then, behold their natural tears?

Do you want them to weep blood from our horses? How will we see their natural tears?

Enter Messenger.

Messenger
The English are embattl'd, you French peers.

The English are ready, my French lords.

Constable

To horse, you gallant princes! straight to horse!Do but behold yon poor and starved band,And your fair show shall suck away their souls,Leaving them but the shales and husks of men.There is not work enough for all our hands;Scarce blood enough in all their sickly veinsTo give each naked curtle-axe a stain,That our French gallants shall to-day draw out,And sheathe for lack of sport. Let us but blow on them,The vapour of our valour will o'erturn them.'Tis positive 'gainst all exceptions, lords,That our superfluous lackeys and our peasants,Who in unnecessary action swarmAbout our squares of battle, were enowTo purge this field of such a hilding foe,Though we upon this mountain's basis byTook stand for idle speculation,But that our honours must not. What's to say?A very little little let us do,And all is done. Then let the trumpets soundThe tucket sonance and the note to mount;For our approach shall so much dare the fieldThat England shall crouch down in fear and yield.

To your horses, you gallant princes! Straight to your horses! Look upon the poor and starved band of men. Your appearance will suck away their souls, leaving them just empty shells of men. There isn't enough work for all of us or enough blood in all their veins to stain one of our axes. Let's just blow on them and watch our breath knock them down. It's true our peasants and servants are enough to purge the battlefield of our enemy. We stand here for them to see, but that doesn't honor us. So, let's do the little that must be done. Then let the trumpets play to announce our approach and watch England crouch down in fear and give up.

Grandpre

Why do you stay so long, my lords of France?Yond island carrions, desperate of their bones,Ill-favouredly become the morning field.Their ragged curtains poorly are let loose,And our air shakes them passing scornfully.Big Mars seems bankrupt in their beggar'd host,And faintly through a rusty beaver peeps;The horsemen sit like fixed candlesticksWith torch-staves in their hand; and their poor jadesLob down their heads, drooping the hides and hips,The gum down-roping from their pale-dead eyes,And in their pale dull mouths the gimmal bitLies foul with chew'd grass, still, and motionless;And their executors, the knavish crows,Fly o'er them, all impatient for their hour.Description cannot suit itself in wordsTo demonstrate the life of such a battle,In life so lifeless as it shows itself.

Enter Grandpre.

Why are you still here, my lords? The poor English are already on the field. Their ragged flags are flying as French air blows them about scornfully. Mars, the god of war, will not spend much on this battle. The horsemen look through their rusty helmets like frozen sticks. With torches in their hands, they sit on horses whose heads hang low showing the bones of their hips as they tug at the grass. The crows are flying high impatiently waiting their deaths. There aren't any words in life to describe this lifeless battle.

Constable

They have said their prayers, and they stay for death.

They have said their prayers and they are ready for death.

Dauphin

Shall we go send them dinners and fresh suitsAnd give their fasting horses provender,And after fight with them?

Should we send them food and new armor, or give their horses provisions before we fight them?

Constable

I stay but for my guard; on to the field!I will the banner from a trumpet take,And use it for my haste. Come, come, away!The sun is high, and we outwear the day.

I'm waiting on my banner man, but never mind. To the field! I will take the banner from a trumpeter. Let's hurry. Come on! The sun is high and we are wasting daylight.

Exit.

Scene III: The English camp.

Enter Gloucester, Bedford, Exeter, Erpingham, with his entire host: Salisbury and Westmoreland.

Gloucester
Where is the King?

Where is the king?

Bedford
The King himself is rode to view their battle.

He has ridden to see the battle for himself.

Westmoreland
Of fighting men they have full three-score thousand.

They have three thousand fighting men.

Exeter
There's five to one; besides, they all are fresh.

That's five to one, and they are all fresh.

Salisbury
God's arm strike with us! 'tis a fearful odds.God be wi' you, princes all; I'll to my charge.If we no more meet till we meet in heaven,Then, joyfully, my noble Lord of Bedford,My dear Lord Gloucester, and my good Lord Exeter,And my kind kinsman, warriors all, adieu!

God be with us! These are fearsome odds. God be with you, princes. I'm going to my men. If we don't meet again until heaven then, know I consider you all, Bedford, Gloucester, Exeter, warriors! Goodbye!

Bedford
Farewell, good Salisbury, and good luck go with thee!

Farewell, Salisbury, and good luck!

Exeter
Farewell, kind lord; fight valiantly to-day!And yet I do thee wrong to mind thee of it,For thou art fram'd of the firm truth of valour.

Goodbye, kind lord. Fight valiantly today, and although I don't have to tell you, you are the epitome of courage.

Bedford
He is as full of valour as of kindness,Princely in both.

Exit Salisbury.

He is as courageous as he is kind.

Enter the King.

Westmoreland
O that we now had hereBut one ten thousand of those men in EnglandThat do no work to-day!

Oh, I wish we had one ten-thousandth of the men in England who have no work today!

King

What's he that wishes so?My cousin Westmoreland? No, my fair cousin.If we are mark'd to die, we are enowTo do our country loss; and if to live,The fewer men, the greater share of honour.God's will! I pray thee, wish not one man more.By Jove, I am not covetous for gold,Nor care I who doth feed upon my cost;It yearns me not if men my garments wear;Such outward things dwell not in my desires;But if it be a sin to covet honour,I am the most offending soul alive.No, faith, my coz, wish not a man from England.God's peace! I would not lose so great an honourAs one man more, methinks, would share from meFor the best hope I have. O, do not wish one more!Rather proclaim it, Westmoreland, through my host,That he which hath no stomach to this fight,Let him depart. His passport shall be made,And crowns for convoy put into his purse.We would not die in that man's companyThat fears his fellowship to die with us.This day is call'd the feast of Crispian.He that outlives this day, and comes safe home,Will stand a tip-toe when this day is named,And rouse him at the name of Crispian.He that shall live this day, and see old age,Will yearly on the vigil feast his neighbours,And say, "To-morrow is Saint Crispian."Then will he strip his sleeve and show his scars,And say, "These wounds I had on Crispian's day."Old men forget; yet all shall be forgot,But he'll remember with advantagesWhat feats he did that day. Then shall our names,Familiar in his mouth as household words,Harry the King, Bedford, and Exeter,Warwick and Talbot, Salisbury and Gloucester,Be in their flowing cups freshly rememb'red.This story shall the good man teach his son;And Crispin Crispian shall ne'er go by,From this day to the ending of the world,But we in it shall be remembered,We few, we happy few, we band of brothers.For he to-day that sheds his blood with meShall be my brother; be he ne'er so vile,This day shall gentle his condition;And gentlemen in

What is the kind of person who makes such a wish? My cousin, Westmoreland? No, my cousin, if we are to die, we are enough and our country doesn't lose anymore men. If we live, then we share more honor. God's will is what I pray. By God, I do not want any gold. I don't care who feeds off my demise. It doesn't bother me, if people borrow my clothes. I am not a material man. But, if it's a sin to want honor, then I am the most sinful soul alive. No, I swear, my cuz, I don't wish for any more men from England. God's peace! I don't want to lose honor in the eyes of my men, so if anyone doesn't wish to fight, let him leave. Tell them, Westmoreland, a passport will be made and money will be provided for the voyage home. Today is the Feast of Saint Crispian, and anyone who lives to see this day will stand tall in the future. He who lives today, and sees old age will tell everyone about the scars he received on Saint Crispian's Day. He'll never forget what feats he accomplished this day. Our names will be engraved in his memory, Harry the King, Bedford and Exeter, Warwick and Talbot, Salisbury and Gloucester. Today will make a story he will tell his son. From now on, the Feast of Saint Crispian will never pass that we won't be remembered. We few, we happy few, we band of brothers. Any who sheds his blood with me will be my brother, no matter how awful. This day will make him anew. Gentlemen, men in their beds in England will wish they were here and consider themselves lesser men compared to any who fought with us today.

England now a-bedShall think themselves accurs'd they were not here,And hold their manhoods cheap whiles any speaksThat fought with us upon Saint Crispin's day.

Salisbury

My sovereign lord, bestow yourself with speed.The French are bravely in their battles set,And will with all expedience charge on us.

Re-enter Salisbury.

My sovereign lord, come quickly. The French are setting up for battle and will soon charge upon us.

King

All things are ready, if our minds be so.

Is everything ready?

Westmoreland

Perish the man whose mind is backward now!

Anyone who isn't may die today!

King

Thou dost not wish more help from England, coz?

You don't wish for more help from England, cuz?

Westmoreland

God's will! my liege, would you and I alone,Without more help, could fight this royal battle!

I only want God's will, my liege! If it were just you and me, we could fight this battle alone!

King

Why, now thou hast unwish'd five thousand men,Which likes me better than to wish us one.You know your places. God be with you all!

Why have you unwished five thousand men for one? You all know your places. God be with you all!

Montjoy

Once more I come to know of thee, King Harry,If for thy ransom thou wilt now compound,Before thy most assured overthrow;For certainly thou art so near the gulf,Thou needs must be englutted. Besides, in mercy,The Constable desires thee thou wilt mindThy followers of repentance; that their soulsMay make a peaceful and a sweet retireFrom off these fields, where, wretches, their poor bodiesMust lie and fester.

Trumpet sounds. Enter Montjoy.

I'm here once more to know what you desire, King Harry. Do you want to negotiate your ransom before you are defeated? You and your men must be in need. Besides, the constable wants to show mercy, and give you an opportunity to retreat from what will soon be your death bed.

King

Who hath sent thee now?

Who sent you this time?

Montjoy

The Constable of France.

King

I pray thee, bear my former answer back:Bid them achieve me and then sell my bones.Good God! why should they mock poor fellows thus?The man that once did sell the lion's skinWhile the beast liv'd, was kill'd with hunting him.A many of our bodies shall no doubtFind native graves, upon the which, I trust,Shall witness live in brass of this day's work;And those that leave their valiant bones in France,Dying like men, though buried in your dunghills,They shall be fam'd; for there the sun shall greet them,And draw their honours reeking up to heaven;Leaving their earthly parts to choke your clime,The smell whereof shall breed a plague in France.Mark then abounding valour in our English,That being dead, like to the bullet's grazing,Break out into a second course of mischief,Killing in relapse of mortality.Let me speak proudly: tell the ConstableWe are but warriors for the working-day.Our gayness and our gilt are all besmirch'dWith rainy marching in the painful field;There's not a piece of feather in our host--Good argument, I hope, we will not fly--And time hath worn us into slovenry;But, by the mass, our hearts are in the trim;And my poor soldiers tell me, yet ere nightThey'll be in fresher robes, or they will pluckThe gay new coats o'er the French soldiers' headsAnd turn them out of service. If they do this--As, if God please, they shall,--my ransom thenWill soon be levied. Herald, save thou thy labour.Come thou no more for ransom, gentle herald.They shall have none, I swear, but these my joints;Which if they have as I will leave 'em them,Shall yield them little, tell the Constable.

Montjoy

I shall, King Harry. And so fare thee well;Thou never shalt hear herald any more.

The Constable of France.

Please take my answer back. Tell them to come and get me. Then they can sell my bones. Good God, why do they mock us this way? The man, who tried to sell the lion's skin before he was dead, was killed while hunting him. Many of us will die today, but they will be honored in heaven, while their dead bodies choke up the air and breed a deadly plague in France. Remember our valor and or ability to cause trouble even with our death. Let me be clear. Tell the constable we are only warriors for today. We don't want peace and we won't surrender. Our bodies may be worn, but our hearts our healthy. My poor soldiers tell me, they will be in fresh clothes tonight, or they will take the new coats over the French soldiers' heads. If they succeed, God willing, my ransom will be known. Montjoy, save yourself some work. Don't come anymore for my ransom. They can have my bones and nothing else. Tell the constable

I will, King Harry. Goodbye. You will never hear from me again.

Exit.

King

I fear thou'lt once more come again for ransom.

I fear he will come once more.

Enter York.

York

My lord, most humbly on my knee I begThe leading of the vaward.

My lord, I beg you, on bended knee, to let me lead the vanguard.

King

Take it, brave York. Now, soldiers, march away;And how thou pleasest, God, dispose the day!

Take it, brave York. Now, soldiers, march. God's will be done.

Exit.

Scene IV: The field of battle.

Alarm. Excursions. Enter Pistol, French Soldier, and Boy.

Pistol
Yield, cur!   *Stop, dog!*

French Soldier
Je pense que vous etes le gentilhomme de bonne   *You are a gentleman with high ranks.*
qualite.

Pistol
Qualitie calmie custure me! Art thou a   *Are you a gentleman? What is your name? Tell*
gentleman?What is thy name? Discuss.   *me.*

French Soldier
O Seigneur Dieu!   *Oh, Seigneur Dieu!*

Pistol
O, Signieur Dew should be a gentleman.Perpend   *Oh, Signieur Dew, be a gentleman and pardon*
my words, O Signieur Dew, and mark:O   *my words. You will be killed with my sword,*
Signieur Dew, thou diest on point of fox,Except,   *unless you pay me for your ransom.*
O signieur, thou do give to meEgregious
ransom.

French Soldier
O, prenez misericorde! ayez pitie de moi!   *O, prenez miericord! Ayez pitie de moi! Have*
                                                   mercy! Have pity on me!

Pistol
Moy shall not serve; I will have forty moys,Or I   *Moy is not enough. You must pay me forty moys,*
will fetch thy rim out at thy throatIn drops of   *or I will cut your throat.*
crimson blood.

French Soldier
Est-il impossible d'echapper la force de ton   *Est-il impossible d'echapper la force de ton*
bras?   *bras? It is impossible. May I escape your arms?*

Pistol
Brass, cur!Thou damned and luxurious   *Brass, you dog! You're just a mountain goat*
mountain goat,Offer'st me brass?   *offering me brass.*

French Soldier
O pardonnez moi!   *O pardonnez moi! Pardon me!*

Pistol
Say'st thou me so? Is that a ton of moys?Come   *Is that a ton of moys? Come here, boy. Ask this*

hither, boy; ask me this slave in FrenchWhat is his name.

slave in French for his name.

Boy

Ecoutez: comment etes-vous appele?

Ecoutez: comment etes-vous appele? Look, what's your name?

French Soldier

Monsieur le Fer.

Monsieur le Fer.

Boy

He says his name is Master Fer.

He says his name is Master Fer.

Pistol

Master Fer! I'll fer him, and firk him, and ferret him.Discuss the same in French unto him.

Master Fer! I'm about to fer him, and firk him. Tell him in French.

Boy

I do not know the French for fer, and ferret, and firk.

I don't know how.

Pistol

Bid him prepare; for I will cut his throat.

Tell him to prepare for death. I'm going to cut his throat.

French Soldier

Que dit-il, monsieur?

Que dit-il, monsieur? What is he saying, sir?

Boy

Il me commande a vous dire que vous faites vous pret; carce soldat ici est dispose tout a cette heure de couper votre gorge.

He told me to tell you to prepare to die. He is about to cut your throat.

Pistol

Owy, cuppele gorge, permafoy,Peasant, unless thou give me crowns, brave crowns;Or mangled shalt thou be by this my sword.

Yes, cut your throat, by God, unless you give me crowns and lots of them. Or you will be mangled by my sword.

French Soldier

O, je vous supplie, pour l'amour de Dieu, me pardonner!Je suis gentilhomme de bonne maison; gardez ma vie, etje vous donnerai deux cents ecus.

Oh, I'm begging you, for the love of God, spare me! I am a gentleman from a good family. Spare me and I will give you two hundred ecus.

Pistol

What are his words?

What did he say?

Boy
He prays you to save his life. He is a gentleman of a good house; and for his ransom he will give you two hundredcrowns.

He begs you to spare his life. He is a gentleman of a good family and he is willing to give you two hundred crowns for his life.

Pistol
Tell him my fury shall abate, and IThe crowns will take.

Tell him I'll take the money.

French Soldier
Petit monsieur, que dit-il?

Young man, what does he say?

Boy
Encore qu'il est contre son jurement de pardonner aucunprisonnier; neanmoins, pour les ecus que vous l'avez promis, il est content de vous donner la liberte, le franchisement.

He says it would be breaking an oath to pardon any prisoner. However, for the money, he is willing to free you.

French Soldier
Sur mes genoux je vous donne mille remercimens; et je m'estime heureux que je suis tombe entre les mains d'un chevalier, je pense, le plus brave, vaillant, et tres distingue seigneurd'Angleterre.

Thank you, thank you! I am lucky to have fallen into the hands of a knight, the most noble gentleman of England.

Pistol
Expound unto me, boy.

Tell me what he said.

Boy
He gives you upon his knees, a thousand thanks; and he esteems himself happy that he hath fallen into the hands of one, as he thinks, the most brave, valorous, and thrice-worthy signieur of England.

He thanks you and considers you the bravest Englishman.

Pistol
As I suck blood, I will some mercy show.Follow me!

As I bleed him dry, I will show some mercy, today. Follow me!

Boy
Suivez-vous le grand capitaine.

Follow the captain.

Exit Pistol and French Soldier.

I did never know so full a voice issue from so

I never heard a voice with so much sense from

empty a heart; but the saying is true, "The empty vessel makes the greatest sound." Bardolph and Nym had ten times more valour than this roaring devil i' the old play, that every one may pare his nails with a wooden dagger; and they are both hang'd; and so would this be, if he durst steal anything adventurously. I must stay with the lackeys with the luggage of our camp. The French might have a good prey of us, if he knew of it; for there is none to guard it but boys.

such an empty heart. The saying, "The empty vessel makes the greatest sound," must be true. Bardolph and Num had ten times more valor than this raging devil. They are both hanged and so will he, if he steals anything. I must stay with the servants and the camp's luggage. The French could make good prey of us if they knew.

Exit.

Scene V: Another part of the field.

Enter Constable, Orleans, Bourbon, Dauphin, and Rambures.

Constable
O diable!

Oh, hell!

Orleans
O Seigneur! le jour est perdu, tout est perdu!

Oh Lord, the day is lost! All is lost!

Dauphin
Mort de ma vie! all is confounded, all!Reproach and everlasting shameSits mocking in our plumes.

Everything is messed up! Shame upon all our heads. Oh good luck, don't run away.

A short alarm.

Constable
Why, all our ranks are broke.

All our men are broken up.

Dauphin
O perdurable shame! let's stab ourselves,Be these the wretches that we play'd at dice for?

Oh, lasting shame! Let's kill ourselves. Are these the same wretches we were gambling on?

Orleans
Is this the king we sent to for his ransom?

Is this the king we questioned about his ransom?

Bourbon
Shame and eternal shame, nothing but shame!Let's die in honour! Once more back again!And he that will not follow Bourbon now,Let him go hence, and with his cap in hand,Like a base pandar, hold the chamber doorWhilst by a slave, no gentler than my dog,His fairest daughter is contaminated.

Shame, shame, and more shame! Let's die with honor. Let's go back once again. Anyone who will not return with me can back with his hat in his hand and stand by the bedroom door of his daughter being taken by a slave.

Constable
Disorder, that hath spoil'd us, friend us now!Let us on heaps go offer up our lives.

We need order! Let's go together, if we must die.

Orleans
We are enow yet living in the fieldTo smother up the English in our throngs,If any order might be thought upon.

We are not enough to take England, if you want to talk about order.

Bourbon
The devil take order now! I'll to the throng.Let

To hell with order, now! I'll go into battle. Let

99

life be short, else shame will be too long.

life be short or shame will be too long.

Exit.

Scene VI: Another part of the field.

Trumpets sound. Enter King Henry and forces, Exeter, and others.

King

Well have we done, thrice valiant countrymen.But all's not done; yet keep the French the field.

We have done well, my valiant countrymen. But, we are not finished with the French still on the field.

Exeter

The Duke of York commends him to your Majesty.

The Duke of York wanted me to send you his regards.

King

Lives he, good uncle? Thrice within this hourI saw him down; thrice up again, and fighting.From helmet to the spur all blood he was.

He is still alive, good uncle? I saw him three times within the hour. He was down, then up and fighting again. He was covered from head to toe in blood.

Exeter

In which array, brave soldier, doth he lie,Larding the plain; and by his bloody side,Yoke-fellow to his honour-owing wounds,The noble Earl of Suffolk also lies.Suffolk first died; and York, all haggled over,Comes to him, where in gore he lay insteeped,And takes him by the beard; kisses the gashesThat bloodily did yawn upon his face.He cries aloud, "Tarry, my cousin Suffolk!My soul shall thine keep company to heaven;Tarry, sweet soul, for mine, then fly abreast,As in this glorious and well-foughten fieldWe kept together in our chivalry."Upon these words I came and cheer'd him up.He smil'd me in the face, raught me his hand,And, with a feeble gripe, says, "Dear my lord,Commend my service to my sovereign."So did he turn and over Suffolk's neckHe threw his wounded arm and kiss'd his lips;And so espous'd to death, with blood he seal'dA testament of noble-ending love.The pretty and sweet manner of it forc'dThose waters from me which I would have stopp'd;But I had not so much of man in me,And all my mother came into mine

The brave soldier lies wounded in the field beside the noble Earl of Suffolk. As Suffolk died, York went over and took him by the beard and kissed his cuts and cried, "Wait, dear cousin Suffolk? My soul will keep yours company on the way to heaven. Wait, sweet soul, we will fly as we fought, side-by-side." I went to him while he was talking to cheer him up. He smiled at me and took my hand and with a feeble grip said, "Commend me to the king." Then he turned and threw his wounded arm over Suffolk's neck and kissed his lips. With noble love, his life ended. I couldn't help but cry.

eyesAnd gave me up to tears.

King

I blame you not;For, hearing this, I must perforce compoundWith mistful eyes, or they will issue too.

I don't blame you, because after hearing this I must hold my tears back.

Trumpet sounds.

But hark! what new alarum is this same?The French have reinforc'd their scatter'd men.Then every soldier kill his prisoners;Give the word through.

Listen! What new alarm is this? The French have brought in reinforcements. Let our men kill their prisoners. Go tell them.

Exit.

Scene VII: Another part of the field.

Enter Fluellen and Gower.

Fluellen
Kill the poys and the luggage! 'Tis expressly against thelaw of arms. 'Tis as arrant a piece of knavery, mark you now, as can be offer't; in your conscience, now, is it not?

Gower
'Tis certain there's not a boy left alive; and the cowardly rascals that ran from the battle ha' done this slaughter.Besides, they have burned and carried away all that was in the King's tent; wherefore the King, most worthily, hath caus'd every soldier to cut his prisoner's throat. O, 'tis a gallant king!

Fluellen
Ay, he was porn at Monmouth, Captain Gower. What call youthe town's name where Alexander the Pig was born?

Gower
Alexander the Great.

Fluellen
Why, I pray you, is not pig great? The pig, or the great, or the mighty, or the huge, or the magnanimous, are all one reckonings, save the phrase is a little variations.

Gower
I think Alexander the Great was born in Macedon. His father was called Philip of Macedon, as I take it.

Fluellen
I think it is in Macedon where Alexander is porn. I tell you, Captain, if you look in the maps of the 'orld, I warrant you sall find, in the comparisons between Macedon and Monmouth, that the situations, look you, is both alike. There is a river in Macedon; and there is also

They killed the boys with the luggage? It's against the law or war. I think it's villainous. Don't you?

It's certain no boy is left alive and the cowards that ran from the battle performed the slaughter. They also burned and carried away all that was in the king's tent, so the king's called for all prisoners to be executed. He's such a gallant king!

Yes, he was born at Monmouth, Captain Gower. What's the name of the where Alexander the Pig was born?

Alexander the Great.

Isn't that the same thing?

I think he was born in Macedon. His father was Philip of Macedon, I think.

I think it is Macedon. Macedon and Monmouth are very similar if you look at a map. They both have rivers. Wye river is in Monmouth, but I can't remember what the other river is. If you compare Alexander's and Harry's lives, they are not very different. God knows, you know, in

moreover a river at Monmouth; it is call'd Wye at Monmouth; but it is out of my prains what is the name of the other river; but 'tis all one, 'tis alike as my fingers is to my fingers, and there is salmons in both. If you mark Alexander's life well, Harry of Monmouth's life is come after it indifferent well; for there is figures in all things. Alexander, God knows, and you know, in his rages, and his furies, and his wraths, and his cholers, and his moods, and his displeasures, and his indignations, and also being a little intoxicates in his prains, did, in his ales and his angers, look you, kill his best friend, Cleitus.

his anger and bad moods, along with ale, Alexander killed his best friend, Cleitus.

Gower

Our King is not like him in that. He never kill'd any of his friends.

Our king is not like him in that. He never killed any of his friends.

Fluellen

It is not well done, mark you now, to take the tales out of my mouth, ere it is made and finished. I speak but in the figures and comparisons of it. As Alexander kill'd his friend Cleitus, being in his ales and his cups; so also Harry Monmouth, being in his right wits and his good judgements, turn'd away the fat knight with the great belly doublet. He was full of jests, and gipes, and knaveries, and mocks; I have forgot his name.

It's not nice to take think you know what I'm saying before I finish. I'm only comparing the two. Alexander, drunk and angry, killed his friend Cleitus, like Harry, smart and wise, turned away that fat knight who was full of jokes and mischief. I have forgotten his name.

Gower

Sir John Falstaff.

Sir John Falstaff.

Fluellen

That is he. I'll tell you there is good men porn at Monmouth.

That's him. There are good men born at Monmouth, I'll tell you.

Gower

Here comes his Majesty.

Here comes his majesty.

Trumpet sounds. Enter King Henry, and forces; Warwick, Gloucester, Exeter, and others.

King

I was not angry since I came to France Until this instant. Take a trumpet, herald; Ride thou

I was not angry when I came to France, until now. Take a trumpet and herald and ride up to unto the horsemen on yond hill. If they will

fight with us, bid them come down,Or void the field; they do offend our sight.If they'll do neither, we will come to them,And make them skirr away, as swift as stonesEnforced from the old Assyrian slings.Besides, we'll cut the throats of those we have,And not a man of them that we shall takeShall taste our mercy. Go and tell them so.

the horseman on the hill, and tell them if they want fight, bring it on, or get away from the field. If they won't do either, we will go to them, and make them run as swift as stones thrown from Assyrian slings. In addition, tell them we're going to execute the men we have. No Frenchmen will have mercy. Go tell them.

Exeter
Here comes the herald of the French, my liege.

Enter Montjoy.

Here comes the herald of the French, my king.

Gloucester
His eyes are humbler than they us'd to be.

He looks more humble than before.

King
How now! what means this, herald? Know'st thou notThat I have fin'd these bones of mine for ransom?Com'st thou again for ransom?

Hey! What now, herald? Don't you know these fine bones are not for ransom? Have you come again?

Montjoy
No, great King;I come to thee for charitable license,That we may wander o'er this bloody fieldTo book our dead, and then to bury them;To sort our nobles from our common men.For many of our princes--woe the while!-- Lie drown'd and soak'd in mercenary blood;So do our vulgar drench their peasant limbsIn blood of princes; and their wounded steedsFret fetlock deep in gore, and with wild rageYerk out their armed heels at their dead masters,Killing them twice. O, give us leave, great King,To view the field in safety, and disposeOf their dead bodies!

No, great king. I come to you for your charity. We would like to look over this bloody field for our dead so we may bury them. We would like to sort our nobles from the common men because there are many princes dead in the field. We would also like to get the horses that are on the field stomping the bodies. Please let us onto the field, great king, to find the bodies and bury them.

King
I tell thee truly, herald,I know not if the day be ours or no;For yet a many of your horsemen peerAnd gallop o'er the field.

I tell you, herald, I don't know if the day is ours. Many of your friends still ride in the field.

Montjoy
The day is yours.

King
Praised be God, and not our strength, for

The day is yours.

Praise be to God. What is that castle called?

it! What is this castle call'd that stands hard by?

Montjoy
They call it Agincourt.

King
Then call we this the field of Agincourt, Fought on the day of Crispin Crispianus.

Fluellen
Your grandfather of famous memory, an't please your Majesty, and your great-uncle Edward the Plack Prince of Wales, as I have read in the chronicles, fought a most prave pattle here in France.

King
They did, Fluellen.

Fluellen
Your Majesty says very true. If your Majesties is rememb'red of it, the Welshmen did good service in garden where leeks did grow, wearing leeks in their Monmouth caps; which, your Majesty know, to this hour is an honourable badge of the service; and I do believe your Majesty takes no scorn to wear the leek upon Saint Tavy's day.

King
I wear it for a memorable honour; For I am Welsh, you know, good countryman.

Fluellen
All the water in Wye cannot wash your Majesty's Welsh plood out of your pody, I can tell you that. Got pless it and preserve it, as long as it pleases His grace, and His majesty too!

King
Thanks, good my countryman.

Fluellen

They call it Agincourt.

Then we will call this the field of Agincourt, and the battle was fought on the day of Crispin Crispianus.

Your grandfather and your great-uncle Edward the Black Prince of Wales, as I have read, fought a most brave battle here in France.

They did, Fluellen.

If I remember correctly, the Welshmen fought bravely in a garden where they grew leeks. Now wearing leeks in Monmouth caps is a badge of honor. I believe you wear a leek on Saint Davy's Day, your Majesty.

I wear it to honor their memory. You know I am Welsh.

All the water in the Wye could not wash out your majesty's Welsh blood. May God bless it and keep it safe, as long as it pleases Him and your majesty!

Thanks, my good countryman.

By Jeshu, I am your Majesty's countryman, I care not who know it. I will confess it to all the 'orld. I need not be asham'd of your Majesty, praised be God, so long as your Majesty is an honest man.

King
God keep me so! Our heralds go with him;Bring me just notice of the numbers deadOn both our parts. Call yonder fellow hither.

Exeter
Soldier, you must come to the King.

King
Soldier, why wear'st thou that glove in thy cap?

Williams
An't please your Majesty, 'tis the gage of one that Ishould fight withal, if he be alive.

King
An Englishman?

Williams
An't please your Majesty, a rascal that swagger'd with melast night; who, if alive and ever dare to challenge thisglove, I have sworn to take him a box o' the ear; or if I can see my glove in his cap, which he swore, as he was a soldier, he would wear if alive, I will strike it out soundly.

King
What think you, Captain Fluellen? Iis it fit this soldier keep his oath?

Fluellen
He is a craven and a villain else, an't please your Majesty, in my conscience.

King
It may be his enemy is a gentlemen of great sort, quite from the answer of his degree.

Fluellen

By God, I am your majesty's countryman. I don't care who knows it. I will confess it to the world. I don't need to be ashamed of your majesty as long as he is an honest man.

May God keep me that way. Heralds go with Montjoy. Find out how many are dead, both English and French. Tell him to come here.

Points to Williams. Exit Heralds with Montjoy.

Soldier, you must come to the king.

Soldier, why are wearing that glove in your cap?

If it pleases you your majesty, it's the glove of a man I will fight, if I ever see him alive again.

An Englishman?

It was a rascal that argued with me last night, who if I see alive again have sworn to give him a knock up against his head. Or, if I see my glove in his cap, which he swore as a soldier he would, I will knock him in the head.

What do you think, Captain Fluellen? Is it proper for this soldier to keep his oath?

He would be crazy and a villain not to, if I may say so.

It may be his enemy is a gentleman beyond reproach.

Though he be as good a gentleman as the devil is, as Lucifier and Belzebub himself, it is necessary, look your Grace, that he keep his vow and his oath. If he be perjur'd, see you now, his reputation is as arrant a villain and a Jacksauce, as ever his black shoe trod upon God's ground and His earth, in myconscience, la!

He may be as good a gentleman as the devil or Lucifer and Beelzebub, but it is necessary for him to keep his oath or be considered a liar or worse, a villain.

King
Then keep thy vow, sirrah, when thou meet'st the fellow.

Then keep your vow, sir, when you meet the fellow.

Williams
So I will, my liege, as I live.

I will, my liege, I swear on my life.

King
Who serv'st thou under?

Who do you serve under?

Williams
Under Captain Gower, my liege.

Captain Gower, my liege.

Fluellen
Gower is a good captain, and is good knowledge andliteratured in the wars.

Gower is a good captain, very knowledgeable in the art of war.

King
Call him hither to me, soldier.

Call him to me, soldier.

Williams
I will, my liege.

I will, my liege.

Exit.

King
Here, Fluellen; wear thou this favour for me and stick it in thy cap. When Alencon and myself were down together, I pluck'd this glove from his helm. If any man challenge this, he is a friend to Alencon, and an enemy to our person. If thou encounter any such, apprehend him, an thou dost me love.

Here Fluellen, wear this in your cap as a favor for me. I took this glove from Alencon when we were down together. If any man challenges this he is a friend to Alencon, and our enemy. If you encounter anyone like this, arrest him, if you love me.

Fluellen
Your Grace doo's me as great honours as can be desir'd in the hearts of his subjects. I would fain

It would be an honor. I would like to find any man with two legs who would take offense at

see the man, that has but two legs, that shall find himself aggrief'd at this glove; that is all. But I would fain see it once, an please God of His grace that I might see.

this glove. I would hate to see it just once, and I hope I do, God willing.

King
Know'st thou Gower?

Do you know Gower?

Fluellen
He is my dear friend, an please you.

He is my dear friend, if it pleases you.

King
Pray thee, go seek him, and bring him to my tent.

Then I ask you to go find him and bring him to my tent.

Fluellen
I will fetch him.

I will.

Exit.

King
My Lord of Warwick, and my brother Gloucester,Follow Fluellen closely at the heels.The glove which I have given him for a favourMay haply purchase him a box o' the ear.It is the soldier's; I by bargain shouldWear it myself. Follow, good cousin Warwick.If that the soldier strike him, as I judgeBy his blunt bearing he will keep his word,Some sudden mischief may arise of it;For I do know Fluellen valiantAnd, touch'd with choler, hot as gunpowder,And quickly will return an injury.Follow, and see there be no harm between them.Go you with me, uncle of Exeter.

My Lord of Warwick and my brother, Gloucester, follow Fluellen. The glove I gave him may get him a knock on the head. It's the soldier's. I should wear it myself. Follow him, good cousin Warwick, and if that soldier follows his oath make sure no harm comes to them. You go with me, Uncle Exeter.

Exit.

Scene VIII: Before King Henry's pavilion.

Enter Gower and Williams.

Williams

I warrant it is to knight you, Captain.

I warn you it is knight to you, captain.

Enter Fluellen.

Fluellen

God's will and his pleasure, captain, I beseech you now, come apace to the King. There is more good toward you peradventure than is in your knowledge to dream of.

God's will, captain, I ask that you come quickly to the king. There is more good for you than you can imagine.

Williams

Sir, know you this glove?

Sir, do you know this glove?

Fluellen

Know the glove! I know the glove is a glove.

Know the glove! I know it's a glove!

Williams

I know this; and thus I challenge it.

I know it and therefore, I challenge you.

Strikes him.

Fluellen

'Sblood! an arrant traitor as any is in the universal world, or in France, or in England!

Hell! You are a wayward traitor as any in the world or in France or in England!

Gower

How now, sir! you villain!

What's going on? You villain!

Williams

Do you think I'll be forsworn?

Did you think I would break my oath?

Fluellen

Stand away, Captain Gower. I will give treason his payment into plows, I warrant you.

Stand back, Captain Gower. I will give him what he's got coming to him. I warn you!

Williams

I am no traitor.

I am no traitor!

Fluellen

That's a lie in thy throat. I charge you in his Majesty's name, apprehend him; he's a friend of the Duke Alencon's.

That's a lie. I charge you in the name of his majesty. Arrest him. He's a friend of the Duke Alencon.

Warwick
How now, how now! what's the matter?

Fluellen
My lord of Warwick, here is--praised be God for it!--a most contagious treason come to light, look you, as you shalldesire in a summer's day. Here is his Majesty.

King
How now! what's the matter?

Fluellen
My liege, here is a villain and a traitor, that, look your Grace, has struck the glove which your Majesty is take out of thehelmet of Alencon.

Williams
My liege, this was my glove; here is the fellow of it; and he that I gave it to in change promis'd to wear it in his cap. I promis'd to strike him, if he did. I met this man with myglove in his cap, and I have been as good as my word.

Fluellen
Your Majesty hear now, saving your Majesty's manhood,what an arrant, rascally, beggarly, lousy knave it is. I hope your Majesty is pear me testimony and witness, and willavouchment, that this is the glove of Alencon that yourMajesty is give me; in your conscience, now?

King
Give me thy glove, soldier. Look, here is the fellow of it. 'Twas I, indeed, thou promisedst to strike;And thou hast given me most bitter terms.

Fluellen
An it please your Majesty, let his neck answer for it, ifthere is any martial law in the world.

Enter Warwick and Gloucester.

Hey! What's the matter?

My Lord of Warwick, praise be to God you are here! A contagious act of treason has come light, bright as a summer's day. Here is his majesty.

Enter King Henry and Exeter.

Hey now! What's the matter?

My liege, here is the villain and traitor that has taken offence at the glove of Alencon.

My liege, this was my glove. Here is the match. The man I gave it to promised me he would wear it in his cap. I promised to strike him, if he did. I met this man with my glove in his cap, and I have kept my word.

Hear me now, your majesty, this is a villain, a rascal, and a beggar. Your majesty, please tell them this is the glove of Alencon that you gave me. Remember?

Give me the glove, soldier. Look, here is the match. I am the man you promised to strike and you have made this difficult for me.

If it pleases your majesty, let's hang him, if there is any law in the world.

113

King
How canst thou make me satisfaction?

How can you make up for this offence?

Williams
All offences, my lord, come from the heart. Never cameany from mine that might offend your Majesty.

All offences, my lord, come from the heart. I never meant to offend you, your majesty.

King
It was ourself thou didst abuse.

You said awful things about me to my face.

Williams
Your Majesty came not like yourself. You appear'd to mebut as a common man; witness the night, your garments, your lowliness; and what your Highness suffer'd under that shape, I beseech you take it for your own fault and not mine; for had you been as I took you for, I made no offence; therefore, I beseech your Highness, pardon me.

You did not come as yourself. You appeared to be a common man. I remember the night, your clothes, your demeanor, and the way you acted. I ask you accept some of the blame because if I had known it was you, I would not have offended you. Please, forgive me.

King
Here, uncle Exeter, fill this glove with crowns,And give it to this fellow. Keep it, fellow;And wear it for an honour in thy capTill I do challenge it. Give him his crowns;And, captain, you must needs be friends with him.

Here, uncle Exeter, fill this glove with crowns and give it to this fellow. Keep it, young man, and wear it for honorably in your cap, until I challenge you for it. Give him the money, and captain, you must be friends with him.

Fluellen
By this day and this light, the fellow has mettle enough in his belly. Hold, there is twelve pence for you; and I pray you to serve God, and keep you out of prawls, and prabbles, andquarrels, and dissensions, and, I warrant you, it is the better for you.

This man is brave enough. Here is twelve pence for you. Go and serve God, I pray. Stay out of trouble and I promise you a long, healthy life.

Williams
I will none of your money.

I don't want any of your money.

Fluellen
It is with a good will; I can tell you, it will serve you to mend your shoes. Come, wherefore should you be so pashful? Your shoes is not so good. 'Tis a good silling, I warrant you, or I will

I want you to have it. Use it to mend your shoes. Don't be filled with pride. Your shoes are no good.

change it.

King
Now, herald, are the dead numb'red?

Herald
Here is the number of the slaught'red French.

King
What prisoners of good sort are taken, uncle?

Exeter
Charles Duke of Orleans, nephew to the King;John Duke of Bourbon, and Lord Bouciqualt:Of other lords and barons, knights and squires,Full fifteen hundred, besides common men.

King
This note doth tell me of ten thousand FrenchThat in the field lie slain; of princes, in this number,And nobles bearing banners, there lie deadOne hundred twenty-six; added to these,Of knights, esquires, and gallant gentlemen,Eight thousand and four hundred; of the which,Five hundred were but yesterday dubb'd knights;So that, in these ten thousand they have lost,There are but sixteen hundred mercenaries;The rest are princes, barons, lords, knights, squires,And gentlemen of blood and quality.The names of those their nobles that lie dead:Charles Delabreth, High Constable of France;Jacques of Chatillon, Admiral of France;The master of the cross-bows, Lord Rambures;Great Master of France, the brave Sir Guichard Dauphin,John Duke of Alencon, Anthony Duke of Brabant,The brother to the Duke of Burgundy,And Edward Duke of Bar; of lusty earls,Grandpre and Roussi, Fauconberg and Foix,Beaumont and Marle, Vaudemont and Lestrale.Here was a royal fellowship of death!Where is the number of our English dead?

Edward the Duke of York, the Earl of

Enter an English Herald.

Herald, how many are dead?

Here is the number of the dead French.

What kind of good prisoners were taken, uncle?

We have Charles Duke of Orleans, nephew to the king, John Duke of Bourbon, and Lord Bouciqualt. We also have about fifteen hundred men, including some lords, barons, knights, squires, and common men.

This tells me out of the ten thousand French who are dead, one hundred twenty-six were nobles bearing banners. Eight thousand, four hundred were knights, squires, and gentlemen. Only five hundred were made knights yesterday. Out of the lost men, sixteen hundred were mercenaries and the rest are princes, barons, lords, knights, squires, and noble men. The dead include, Charles Delabreth, high constable of France; Jaques of Chatillon, admiral of France; the master of cross-bows, Lord Rambures; great master of France, Sir Guichard Dolphin; John, Duke of Alencon; Anthony, Duke of Brabant; the brother of the Duke of Burgundy; and Edward, Duke of Bar. The dead earls are Grandpre, Roussi, Fauconberg, Foix, Beaumont, Marle, Vaudemont, and Lestrale. Here was a royal group of dead! Where is the number of the English casualties?

Herald shows him another paper.

This says Edward, the Duke of York, the Earl of

Suffolk,Sir Richard Ketly, Davy Gam, esquire;None else of name; and of all other menBut five and twenty.--O God, thy arm was here;And not to us, but to thy arm alone,Ascribe we all! When, without stratagem,But in plain shock and even play of battle,Was ever known so great and little lossOn one part and on the other? Take it, God,For it is none but thine!

Exeter
'Tis wonderful!

King
Come, go we in procession to the village;And be it death proclaimed through our hostTo boast of this or take that praise from GodWhich is His only.

Fluellen
Is it not lawful, an please your Majesty, to tell howmany is kill'd?

King
Yes, Captain; but with this acknowledgment,That God fought for us.

Fluellen
Yes, my conscience, He did us great good.

King
Do we all holy rites.Let there be sung Non nobis and Te Deum,The dead with charity enclos'd in clay,And then to Calais; and to England then,Where ne'er from France arriv'd more happy men.

Suffolk, Sir Richard Ketly, and squire Davy Gam. We only lost twenty-five other men. Thank God! Never has another battle tallied such great loss on one side and so little on the other. It was God's work, not mine!

It's wonderful!

Come, let's go together to the village. Death to anyone who takes credit for this victory. To God be the glory.

It's not lawful, if it pleases your majesty, to tell how many are dead?

Yes, captain, but when we acknowledge it, it will show God fought for us.

Yes, I know, he did us great good.

We must observe all holy rites. Sing "Non Nobis" and "Te Deum" Let the dead be buried. Then we must go to Calais and to England. There have never been happier men to return home.

Exit.

Act V

Prologue

Enter Chorus.

Chorus

Vouchsafe to those that have not read the story,That I may prompt them; and of such as have,I humbly pray them to admit the excuseOf time, of numbers, and due course of things,Which cannot in their huge and proper lifeBe here presented. Now we bear the KingToward Calais; grant him there; there seen,Heave him away upon your winged thoughtsAthwart the sea. Behold, the English beachPales in the flood with men, with wives and boys,Whose shouts and claps out-voice the deep-mouth'd sea,Which like a mighty whiffler 'fore the KingSeems to prepare his way. So let him land,And solemnly see him set on to London.So swift a pace hath thought that even nowYou may imagine him upon Blackheath,Where that his lords desire him to have borneHis bruised helmet and his bended swordBefore him through the city. He forbids it,Being free from vainness and self-glorious pride;Giving full trophy, signal, and ostentQuite from himself to God. But now behold,In the quick forge and working-house of thought,How London doth pour out her citizens!The mayor and all his brethren in best sort,Like to the senators of the antique Rome,With the plebeians swarming at their heels,Go forth and fetch their conquering Caesar in;As, by a lower but loving likelihood,Were now the general of our gracious empress,As in good time he may, from Ireland coming,Bringing rebellion broached on his sword,How many would the peaceful city quit,To welcome him! Much more, and much more cause,Did they this Harry. Now in London place him;As yet the lamentation of the FrenchInvites the King of England's stay at home,--The Emperor's

Those of you who have not heard the story, trust me. I beg your pardon for the lack of time and if we have left out any details. We could not present them all. Now, we see the king going toward Calais. Afterwards, see him upon the sea, and then the English beach. Men flood the beach. Wives and boys shout and clap, drowning out the deep, loud sea and preparing the way for the king. Now, he is in London where his lords want to see his dented helmet and bent sword. He forbids it, not being vain and filled with pride. He gives all the credit to God. Behold now the citizens of London pouring out. The mayor and all his constituents swarm at their heels like the senators of ancient Rome to see their Caesar. Imagine the queen returning home from victory in Ireland, and how many people would come out to see him. There were much more to welcome Harry. Now, see him in London, coming home from the mourning of France. The emperor is coming on behalf of France to put order and peace between them. Remember this has taken place as we return to France.

coming in behalf of France,To order peace
between them;--and omitAll the occurrences,
whatever chanc'd,Till Harry's back-return again
to France.There must we bring him; and myself
have play'dThe interim, by rememb'ring you 'tis
past.Then brook abridgment, and your eyes
advanceAfter your thoughts, straight back again
to France.

Exit.

Scene I: France. The English camp.

Enter Fluellen and Gower.

Gower
Nay, that's right; but why wear you your leek to-day?Saint Davy's day is past.

Fluellen
There is occasions and causes why and wherefore in allthings. I will tell you asse my friend, Captain Gower. The rascally, scald, beggarly, lousy, pragging knave, Pistol, which you and yourself and all the world know to be no petter than a fellow, look you now, of no merits, he is come to me and prings me pread and salt yesterday, look you, and bid me eat my leek. It was in a place where I could not breed no contention with him; but I will be so bold as to wear it in my cap till I see him once again, and then I will tell him a little piece of my desires.

Gower
Why, here he comes, swelling like a turkey-cock.

Fluellen
'Tis no matter for his swellings nor his turkey-cocks. God pless you, Aunchient Pistol! you scurvy, lousy knave, Godpless you!

Pistol
Ha! art thou bedlam? Dost thou thirst, base Troyan,To have me fold up Parca's fatal web?Hence! I am qualmish at the smell of leek.

Fluellen
I peseech you heartily, scurfy, lousy knave, at my desires, and my requests, and my petitions, to eat, look you, thisleek. Because, look you, you do not love it, nor youraffections and your appetites and your digestions doo's not agree with it, I would desire you to eat it.

No, that's right, but why are you wearing your leek today? Saint Davy's day has past.

There are reasons for everything. I tell you, Captain Gower, Pistol, that louse rascal, came to me yesterday and brought me bread and salt. He asked me to eat my leek. I was in no place for a fight so, I'm going to wear it in my cap until I see him again. Then, I'm going to give him a piece of my mind.

Enter Pistol.

Well, here he comes, puffed up like a rooster.

This is no matter for his puffiness or bird-like qualities. God bless you, Pistol, you scurvy, lousy man. God bless you!

Ha! Are you crazy? Do you want to fight? Come on! I get sick at the smell of leek.

I ask you to eat this leek, you rascal. If it makes you sick, I really want you to eat it.

Pistol
Not for Cadwallader and all his goats.

Not for Cadwallader and all his goats.

Fluellen
There is one goat for you.

Here is a goat for you.

Strikes him.

Will you be sogood, scald knave, as eat it?

Will you be so good as to eat it, you villain?

Pistol
Base Troyan, thou shalt die.

You will die.

Fluellen
You say very true, scald knave, when God's will is. I willdesire you to live in the mean time, and eat your victuals. Come, there is sauce for it.

When it's God's will. In the meantime, I would like for you to live and eat your food. Come on, here's some sauce for it.

Strikes him.

You call'd meyesterday mountain-squire; but I will make you to-day asquire of low degree. I pray you, fall to; if you can mocka leek, you can eat a leek.

You called me out yesterday, but I will make you a lowly squire today. Now, if you can mock a leek, you can eat one.

GOWER
Enough, captain; you have astonish'd him.

Fluellen
I say, I will make him eat some part of my leek, or I willpeat his pate four days. Bite, I pray you; it is good foryour green wound and your ploody coxcomb.

Go ahead and eat. Would you like some more sauce? There is not enough leek to swear by.

Pistol
Must I bite?

Must I bite it?

Fluellen
Yes, certainly, and out of doubt and out of questiontoo, and ambiguities.

Without a doubt.

Pistol
By this leek, I will most horribly revenge. I eat andeat, I swear--

I swear by this leek, I will get revenge. I swear as I eat it.

Fluellen

Eat, I pray you. Will you have some more sauce toyour leek? There is not enough leek to swear by.

Pistol

Quiet thy cudgel; thou dost see I eat.

Fluellen

Much good do you, scald knave, heartily. Nay, pray you,throw none away; the skin is good for your broken coxcomb.When you take occasions to see leeks herefter, I pray you,mock at 'em; that is all.

Pistol

Good.

Fluellen

Ay, leeks is good. Hold you, there is a groat to healyour pate.

Pistol

Me a groat!

Fluellen

Yes, verily and in truth you shall take it; or I haveanother leek in my pocket, which you shall eat.

Pistol

I take thy groat in earnest of revenge.

Fluellen

If I owe you anything I will pay you in cudgels. Youshall be a woodmonger, and buy nothing of me but cudgels.God be wi' you, and keep you, and heal your pate.

Pistol

All hell shall stir for this.

Gower

Go, go; you are a couterfeit cowardly knave. Will you mockat an ancient tradition, begun upon an honourable respect, and worn as a

Eat it all. Don't throw any away. The skin is good for your broken head. Next time you see leeks, I dare you to mock at them. That's all.

Shut your mouth. I am eating it.

_____
_____
_____
_____

Good.

Yes, leeks are good. Here is some money to heal your wounds.

Money, for me?

Yes. Take it or I have another leek in my pocket for you to eat.

I'll take your money as a reminder of revenge.

If I owe you anything, I'll pay you in beatings. God be with you, keep you safe, and heal your head.

Exit.

All hell will break for this.

Go on. You are a fake, cowardly villain. How dare you mock an ancient tradition steeped in honor, but not back it up with actions? I have

memorable trophy of predeceased valour, and dare not avouch in your deeds any of your words? I have seen you gleeking and galling at this gentleman twice or thrice. You thought, because he could not speak English in the native garb, he could not therefore handle an English cudgel. You find it otherwise; and henceforth let a Welsh correction teach you a good English condition. Fare ye well.

Pistol

Doth Fortune play the huswife with me now?News have I, that my Doll is dead i' the spitalOf malady of France;And there my rendezvous is quite cut off.Old I do wax; and from my weary limbsHonour is cudgell'd. Well, bawd I'll turn,And something lean to cutpurse of quick hand.To England will I steal, and there I'll steal;And patches will I get unto these cudgell'd scars,And swear I got them in the Gallia wars.

seen you mocking this man more than once. You thought, because he could not speak English well, he couldn't handle you. Let this be a lesson to you. Farewell.

Exit.

Is Fortune is playing housewife with me? My Nell has died and she was my last hope. I am getting old and have nothing left. I will return to stealing and my former life. First, I'll steal away to England, and steal some more when I get there. I'll tell everyone these wounds are from the French wars.

Exit.

Scene II: France. A royal palace.

Enter, at one door King Henry, Exeter, Bedford, Gloucester, Warwick, Westmoreland, and other Lords; at another, the French King, Queen Isabel the Princess Katharine, Alice and other Ladies; the Duke of Burgundy and his train.

King

Peace to this meeting, wherefore we are met!Unto our brother France, and to our sister,Health and fair time of day; joy and good wishesTo our most fair and princely cousin Katharine;And, as a branch and member of this royalty,By whom this great assembly is contriv'd,We do salute you, Duke of Burgundy;And, princes French, and peers, health to you all!

May this meeting be peaceful. We wish health to our brother France and good wishes to our sister and Princess Katharine. We salute you, Duke of Burgundy, and wish good health to all the French princes and peers.

French King

Right joyous are we to behold your face,Most worthy brother England; fairly met!So are you, princes English, every one.

We are happy to see you, most worthy brother England and noble English princes.

Queen Isabel

So happy be the issue, brother England,Of this good day and of this gracious meetingAs we are now glad to behold your eyes;Your eyes, which hitherto have borne in themAgainst the French that met them in their bentThe fatal balls of murdering basilisks.The venom of such looks, we fairly hope,Have lost their quality; and that this dayShall change all griefs and quarrels into love.

I salute you, English princes.

Burgundy

My duty to you both, on equal love,Great Kings of France and England! That I have labour'd,With all my wits, my pains, and strong endeavours,To bring your most imperial MajestiesUnto this bar and royal interview,Your mightiness on both parts best can witness.Since then my office hath so far prevail'dThat, face to face and royal eye to eye,You have congreeted, let it not disgrace meIf I demand, before this royal view,What rub or what impediment there is,Why that the

I give my duty to both of you, great kings of France and England! I have worked with everything I am to bring your majesties to this meeting. Since I have accomplished my job, please allow me to ask for peace. Shouldn't France have as much? She has been chased too long and her fertility compromised with disorder. Her once beautiful flowers are dead. Our children grow like soldiers, meditating on death. Everything is in total disarray; therefore, I must ask for peace, so we may return to our naked, poor, and mangled Peace,Dear nurse of arts, plenties, and joyful births,Should not in this best garden of the world,Our fertile France, put up her lovely visage?Alas, she hath from France too long been chas'd,And all her husbandry doth lie on heaps,Corrupting in it own fertility.Her vine, the merry cheerer of the heart,Unpruned dies; her hedges even-pleach'd,Like prisoners wildly overgrown with hair,Put forth disorder'd twigs; her fallow leasThe darnel, hemlock, and rank fumitory,Doth root upon, while that the coulter rustsThat should deracinate such savagery;The even mead, that erst brought sweetly forthThe freckled cowslip, burnet, and green clover,Wanting the scythe, all uncorrected, rank,Conceives by idleness, and nothing teemsBut hateful docks, rough thistles, kexes, burs,Losing both beauty and utility;And as our vineyards, fallows, meads, and hedges,Defective in their natures, grow to wildness.Even so our houses and ourselves and childrenHave lost, or do not learn for want of time,The sciences that should become our country;But grow like savages,--as soldiers willThat nothing do but meditate on blood,--To swearing and stern looks, diffus'd attire,And everything that seems unnatural.Which to reduce into our former favourYou are assembled; and my speech entreatsThat I may know the let, why gentle PeaceShould not expel these inconveniencesAnd bless us with her former qualities.

former state.

King

If, Duke of Burgundy, you would the peace,Whose want gives growth to the imperfectionsWhich you have cited, you must buy that peaceWith full accord to all our just demands;Whose tenours and particular effectsYou have enschedul'd briefly in your hands.

If you would like peace, whose absence has caused these imperfections, all you must do is agree to our just demands.

Burgundy

The King hath heard them; to the which as yetThere is no answer made.

The king has heard them, but he has yet to answer.

King
Well, then, the peace,Which you before so urg'd, lies in his answer.

Well, peace lies in his answer.

French King
I have but with a cursorary eyeO'erglanc'd the articles. Pleaseth your GraceTo appoint some of your council presentlyTo sit with us once more, with better heedTo re-survey them, we will suddenlyPass our accept and peremptory answer.

I have looked over them briefly. If it pleases your grace, I would like to appoint some of your councilmen here to sit with us and go over them again. Then, I will give my answer.

King
Brother, we shall. Go, uncle Exeter,And brother Clarence, and you, brother Gloucester,Warwick, and Huntington, go with the King;And take with you free power to ratify,Augment, or alter, as your wisdoms bestShall see advantageable for our dignity,Anything in or out of our demands,And we'll consign thereto. Will you, fair sister,Go with the princes, or stay here with us?

We will, brother. Go with him, uncle Exeter, brother Clarence, brother Gloucester, Warwick and Huntingdon. You have free reign to accept or change the terms as you see fit. Will you, fair sister, go with the princes, or stay here with us?

Queen Isabel
Our gracious brother, I will go with them.Haply a woman's voice may do some good,When articles too nicely urg'd be stood on.

Our gracious brother, I will go with them. A woman's voice may do some good when they disagree.

King
Yet leave our cousin Katharine here with us:She is our capital demand, compris'dWithin the fore-rank of our articles.

Leave our cousin Katharine here with us. She is our main demand.

Queen Isabel
She hath good leave.

She may stay.

King
Fair Katharine, and most fair,Will you vouchsafe to teach a soldier termsSuch as will

Exit all except Henry, Katharine, and Alice.

Fair Katharine, will you allow me to plead my love for you?

enter at a lady's earAnd plead his love-suit to her gentle heart?

Katharine
Your Majesty shall mock me; I cannot speak yourEngland.

Your majesty, you mock me. I can't speak English.

King
O fair Katharine, if you will love me soundly with yourFrench heart, I will be glad to hear you confess it brokenly with your English tongue. Do you like me, Kate?

If you love me, I don't care if you speak English. Do you like me?

Katharine
Pardonnez-moi, I cannot tell wat is "like me."

Pardon me, I don't know the words "like me."

Henry
An angel is like you, Kate, and you are like an angel.

You are like an angel.

Katharine
Que dit-il? Que je suis semblable a les anges?

What is he saying? I am an angel?

Alice
Oui, vraiment, sauf votre grace, ainsi dit-il.

Yes, your grace, that's what he said.

King
I said so, dear Katharine; and I must not blush to affirm it.

I did, dear Katharine, and I am not ashamed to say it again.

Katharine
O bon Dieu! les langues des hommes sont pleines de tromperies.

Oh, Lord! Men are such liars.

King
What says she, fair one? That the tongues of men are full of deceits?

What did she say? Men are liars?

Alice
Oui, dat de tongues of de mans is be full of deceits: dat is de Princess.

Yes, she said that the tongue of man is full of lies.

King
The Princess is the better Englishwoman. I' faith, Kate, my wooing is fit for thy

She sounds like an Englishwoman. I swear Kate, my love for you is not for you to understand. I

understanding: I am glad thou canstspeak no better English; for if thou couldst, thou wouldstfind me such a plain king that thou wouldst think I had sold my farm to buy my crown. I know no ways to mince it in love, but directly to say, "I love you"; then if you urge me farther than to say, "Do you in faith?" I wear out my suit. Give me your answer; i' faith, do; and so clap hands and a bargain. How say you, lady?

am glad you can't speak English better. If you could, you would see I'm just a plain king, and think I sold my farm to buy my crown. I am not educated in the ways of love. I am too direct in saying "I love you." If I must I will swear it. Tell me what you think.

Katharine
Sauf votre honneur, me understand well.

I think I understand.

King
Marry, if you would put me to verses, or to dance for yoursake, Kate, why you undid me; for the one, I have neitherwords nor measure, and for the other I have no strength inmeasure, yet a reasonable measure in strength. If I could win a lady at leap-frog, or by vaulting into my saddle with my armour on my back, under the correction of bragging be it spoken, I should quickly leap into a wife. Or if I might buffet for my love, or bound my horse for her favours, I could lay on like a butcher and sit like a jack-an-apes, never off. But, before God, Kate, I cannot look greenly, nor gasp out my eloquence, nor I have no cunning in protestation; only downright oaths, which I never use till urg'd, nor never break for urging. If thou canst love a fellow of this temper, Kate, whose face is not worth sunburning, that never looks in his glass for love of anything he sees there, let thine eye be thy cook. I speak to thee plain soldier. If thou canst love me for this, take me; if not, to say to thee that I shall die, is true; but for thy love, by the Lord, no; yet I love thee too. And while thou liv'st, dear Kate, take a fellow of plain and uncoined constancy; for he perforce must do thee right, because he hath not the gift to woo in other places; for these fellows of infinite tongue, that can rhyme themselves into ladies' favours, they do always reason themselves out again. What! a speaker is but a prater: a rhyme is but a ballad. A good leg will fall; a straight back will stoop; a black beard will turn white; a curl'd pate

If you would like for me to write poetry or dance for you, then I am defeated. I am not a writer or a dancer, but I am strong. If I could win a lady at games or by jumping into my saddle in full armor, then I would do so for you. I am just an honest man. If you can love a man like me, look at me. Take me as I am, dear Kate, a plain fellow without any charm. I have a good heart which will remain true to you. If you would have a man like me, take me, take this soldier, take this king. What do you say? Tell me.

will grow bald; a fair face will wither; a full eye will wax hollow; but a good heart, Kate, is the sun and the moon; or rather the sun and not the moon; for it shines bright and never changes, but keeps his course truly. If thou would have such a one, take me; and take me, take a soldier; take a soldier, take a king. And what say'st thou then to my love? Speak, my fair, and fairly, I pray thee.

Katharine
Is it possible dat I should love de enemy of France?

Is it possible for me to love the enemy of France?

King
No; it is not possible you should love the enemy of France, Kate; but, in loving me, you should love the friend of France; for I love France so well that I will not part with a village of it, I will have it all mine; and, Kate, when France is mine and I am yours, then yours is France and you are mine.

No, it's not possible, but in loving me you will love the friend of France. I love France so much I want it for myself, and when France is mine, France is yours.

Katharine
I cannot tell wat is dat.

I don't understand.

King
No, Kate? I will tell thee in French; which I am sure will hang upon my tongue like a new-married wife about her husband'sneck, hardly to be shook off. Je quand sur le possession de France, et quand vous avez le possession de moi,--let me see, what then? Saint Denis be my speed!--donc votre est Franceet vous etes mienne. It is as easy for me, Kate, to conquer the kingdom as to speak so much more French. I shall never move thee in French, unless it be to laugh at me.

I will tell you in French. (In French.) When I own France and you have me...Let me see. Help me, Saint Denis! Then yours is France and you are mine. It would be easier for me to win France than to explain what I'm saying in French. You will laugh at me.

Katharine
Sauf votre honneur, le Francais que vous parlez, il est meilleur que l'Anglois lequel je parle.

Your French is better than my English, sir.

King
No, faith, is't not, Kate; but thy speaking of my

No, not really, Kate. We are about the same.

130

tongue, and I thine, most truly-falsely, must needs be granted to be much at one. But, Kate, dost thou understand thus much English: canst thou love me?

Katharine
I cannot tell.

King
Can any of your neighbours tell, Kate? I'll ask them. Come, I know thou lovest me; and at night, when you come into yourcloset, you'll question this gentlewoman about me; and I know, Kate, you will to her dispraise those parts in me that you love with your heart. But, good Kate, mock me mercifully; therather, gentle princess, because I love thee cruelly. If ever thou beest mine, Kate, as I have a saving faith within me tells me thou shalt, I get thee with scambling, and thou must therefore needs prove a good soldier-breeder. Shall not thou and I, between Saint Denis and Saint George, compound a boy, half French, half English, that shall go to Constantinople and take the Turk by the beard? Shall we not? What say'st thou, my fair flower-de-luce?

Katharine
I do not know dat.

King
No; 'tis hereafter to know, but now to promise. Do but now promise, Kate, you will endeavour for your French part ofsuch a boy; and for my English moiety, take the word of a king and a bachelor. How answer you, la plus belle Katherine du monde, mon tres cher et divin deesse?

Katharine
Your Majestee ave fausse French enough to deceive de mostsage damoiselle dat is en France.

King
Now, fie upon my false French! By mine

Can you understand this? Could you love me?

I don't know, yet.

Do any of your neighbors know, Kate? I'll ask them. You know they love me. At night, in your bedroom, you will tell this gentlewoman about me, what parts you love. Don't mock me too much, because I love you. If you are ever mine, Kate, and I have feeling you will, we will have many sons. If not, I will go to Constantinople and take the Turk by the beard? what do you think, my flower?

I don't know.

Of course not. Promise me you will try to have a son. I will do my part. Believe me. What's your answer, (In French.) my most precious and divine goddess?

Your majesty, your French is well enough to fool the wisest French lady.

Now, damn my pathetic French and I swear in

honour, in true English, I love thee, Kate; by which honour I dare not swear thou lovest me; yet my blood begins to flatter me that thou dost,notwithstanding the poor and untempering effect of my visage. Now, beshrew my father's ambition! he was thinking of civil wars when he got me; therefore was I created with a stubborn outside, with an aspect of iron, that, when I come to woo ladies, I fright them. But, in faith, Kate, the elder I wax, the better I shall appear. My comfort is, that old age, that ill layer up of beauty, can do no more spoil upon my face. Thou hast me, if thou hast me, at the worst; and thou shalt wear me, if thou wear me, better and better; and therefore tell me, most fair Katharine, will you have me? Put off your maiden blushes; avouch the thoughts of your heart with the looks of an empress; take me by the hand, and say, Harry of England, I am thine; which word thou shalt no sooner bless mine ear withal, but I will tell thee aloud, England is thine, Ireland is thine, France is thine, and Henry Plantagenet is thine; who, though I speak it before his face, if he be not fellow with the best king, thou shalt find the best king of good fellows.Come, your answer in broken music; for thy voice is music and thy English broken; therefore, queen of all, Katharine, break thy mind to me in broken English. Wilt thou have me?

English, I love you, Kate. I would not swear you love me, but I feel it in my blood you do. Due to my father's ambition, I was born with a stubborn streak and a look of iron so, when I woo ladies I frighten them. But I believe as I grow older, I will soften up. So, if you will have me at my worst, I swear I will get better. Most fair Katharine, will you have me? Don't be embarrassed. Just tell me what is on your heart. Take my hand and say, "Harry of England, I am yours." As soon as I hear it, I will tell you, "England, Ireland, France, and Harry Plantagenet yours." Let me hear your musical voice in broken English tell me what you think. Will you have me?

Katharine
Dat is as it shall please de roi mon pere.

If it pleases my father, the king.

King
Nay, it will please him well, Kate; it shall please him, Kate.

It will please him well, Kate. It will definitely please him.

Katharine
Den it sall also content me.

Then, it also pleases me.

King
Upon that I kiss your hand, and call you my queen.

Then, I will kiss your hand and call you my queen.

Katharine

Laissez, mon seigneur, laissez, laissez! Ma foi, je ne veux point que vous abaissez votre grandeur en baisant la main d'une indigne serviteur. Excusez-moi, je vous supplie, mon tres-puissant seigneur.

No! Please stop! I can't let you lower yourself by kissing the hand of one of your humble servants. Please pardon me, mighty king.

King

Then I will kiss your lips, Kate.

Then, I will kiss your lips, Kate.

Katharine

Les dames et demoiselles pour etre baisees devant leur noces, il n'est pas la coutume de France.

It is not customary for French girls to kiss before they are married.

King

Madame my interpreter, what says she?

What did she say, madam?

Alice

Dat it is not be de fashion pour les ladies of France,--I cannot tell wat is baiser en Anglish.

It is not appropriate for ladies of France. I don't know the English word for "baiser."

King

To kiss.

Kiss.

Alice

Your Majestee entendre bettre que moi.

You understand better than me.

King

It is not a fashion for the maids in France to kiss before they are married, would she say?

It is not appropriate for ladies in France to kiss before they are married, right?

Alice

Oui, vraiment.

Yes.

King

O Kate, nice customs curtsy to great kings. Dear Kate, you and I cannot be confined within the weak list of a country's fashion. We are the makers of manners, Kate; and the liberty that follows our places stops the mouth of all find-faults, as I will do yours, for upholding the nice fashion of your country in denying me a kiss; therefore, patiently and yielding.

Oh Kate, nice customs bow before great kings. Dear Kate, you and I can't be restrained by a list of a country's customs. We set the customs, Kate, and the freedom goes with our positions to silence any who would criticize, like me when I silence you for upholding the old tradition of refusing me a kiss.

Kisses her.

You have witchcraft in your lips, Kate; there is more eloquence in a sugar touch of them than in the tongues of the French council; and they should sooner persuade Harry of England than a general petition of monarchs. Here comes your father.

Your lips are magical, Kate. There is more eloquence in one touch of them than in all the tongues of the French council. You could persuade Harry of England better than a king. Here comes your father.

Re-enter the French King and his Queen, Burgundy, and other Lords.

Burgundy
God save your Majesty! My royal cousin, teach you our princess English?

God save the king! Are you teaching our princess, English?

King
I would have her learn, my fair cousin, how perfectly I love her; and that is good English.

I would have her learn, my fair cousin, how much I love her. That is good English.

Burgundy
Is she not apt?

How does she feel?

King
Our tongue is rough, coz, and my condition is not smooth; so that, having neither the voice nor the heart of flattery about me, I cannot so conjure up the spirit of love in her, that he will appear in his true likeness.

Our language barrier is rough, cuz, and I not a smooth man. So, having neither the voice nor the art of flattery in me, I can't bring about the spirit of love in her.

Burgundy
Pardon the frankness of my mirth, if I answer you for that. If you would conjure in her, you must make a circle; if conjure up Love in her in his true likeness, he must appear naked and blind. Can you blame her then, being a maid yet ros'd over with the virgin crimson of modesty, if she deny the appearance of a naked blind boy in her naked seeing self? It were, my lord, a hard condition for a maid to consign to.

Pardon me, but if you want to make her love you by Cupid's bow, he must come naked. Since she is just a maiden and a modest virgin, you can't blame her for not wanting him to come. It's hard for a young lady to resign herself to loving a man.

King
Yet they do wink and yield, as love is blind and enforces.

Yet, young girls wink and act coy all the time while love is brewing.

Burgundy
They are then excus'd, my lord, when they see not what they do.

Then they are excused for not knowing what they do, my lord.

King
Then, good my lord, teach your cousin to consent winking.

Then teach your cousin, my lord.

Burgundy
I will wink on her to consent, my lord, if you will teach her to know my meaning; for maids, well summer'd and warm kept, are like flies at Bartholomew-tide, blind, though they have their eyes; and then they will endure handling, which before would not abide looking on.

I will give her a wink to consent, my lord, if you will teach her my meaning. Young girls are like flies at Bartholomew's Eve, when they are blind they are easily handled.

King
This moral ties me over to time and a hot summer; and so I shall catch the fly, your cousin, in the latter end, and she must be blind too.

This moral is to give it time and wait until summer. Then, she must still be blinded by my love for me to catch her.

Burgundy
As love is, my lord, before it loves.

Like love, my lord, before it learns to love.

King
It is so; and you may, some of you, thank love for my blindness, who cannot see many a fair French city for one fair French maid that stands in my way.

Okay. Some of you may wish to thank me because I can't see one fair French city with one fair French maid in my way.

French King
Yes, my lord, you see them perspectively, the cities turn'd into a maid; for they are all girdled with maiden walls that war hath [never] ent'red.

Oh yes you do, my lord. You see cities that appear like maidens because they haven't been touched.

King
Shall Kate be my wife?

Will Kate be my wife?

French King
So please you.

If it pleases you.

King
I am content, so the maiden cities you talk of may wait on her; so the maid that stood in the way for my wish shall show me the way to my will.

I am content to wait upon the cities as long as she comes with them. She is the obstacle and the device to achieving my goals.

French King
We have consented to all terms of reason.

We have agreed to all the reasonable terms.

King

Is't so, my lords of England?

Is it true, my lords of England?

Westmoreland

The king hath granted every article;His daughter first, and then in sequel all,According to their firm proposed natures.

The king has agreed to every article. His daughter first, and then in sequence according to their purposes.

Exeter

Only he hath not yet subscribed this: where your Majesty demands, that the King of France, having any occasion to write for matter of grant, shall name your Highness in this form and with this addition, in French, Notre tres-cher fils Henri, Roi d'Angleterre, Heritier de France; and thus in Latin, Praeclarissimus filius noster Henricus, Rex Angliae et Haeres Franciae.

Although, he has not agreed to call you by your French title, Notre tres cher fils Henri, Roi d'Angleterre, Hertier de France.

French King

Nor this I have not, brother, so deniedBut our request shall make me let it pass.

I am willing to agree to this if you demand it.

King

I pray you then, in love and dear alliance,Let that one article rank with the rest;And thereupon give me your daughter.

Then, I ask you to accept it like the rest and give me your daughter.

French King

Take her, fair son, and from her blood raise upIssue to me; that the contending kingdomsOf France and England, whose very shores look paleWith envy of each other's happiness,May cease their hatred; and this dear conjunctionPlant neighbourhood and Christian-like accordIn their sweet bosoms, that never war advanceHis bleeding sword 'twixt England and fair France.

Take her, my son, and give me grandchildren to look after the contending kingdoms of France and England. I hope it ends the hatred and brings about peace so, we may never fight again.

All

Amen!

Amen!

King

Now, welcome, Kate; and bear me witness all,That here I kiss her as my sovereign queen.

Now, welcome, Kate, and everyone be my witness that I kiss her as my sovereign queen.

Queen Isabel
God, the best maker of all marriages,Combine your hearts in one, your realms in one!As man and wife, being two, are one in love,So be there 'twixt your kingdoms such a spousal,That never may ill office, or fell jealousy,Which troubles oft the bed of blessed marriage,Thrust in between the paction of these kingdoms,To make divorce of their incorporate league;That English may as French, French Englishmen,Receive each other. God speak this Amen!

All
Amen!

King
Prepare we for our marriage; on which day,My Lord of Burgundy, we'll take your oath,And all the peers', for surety of our leagues,Then shall I swear to Kate, and you to me;And may our oaths well kept and prosperous be!

Epilogue

Chorus
Thus far, with rough and all-unable pen,Our bending author hath pursu'd the story,In little room confining mighty men,Mangling by starts the full course of their glory.Small time, but in that small most greatly livedThis star of England. Fortune made his sword,By which the world's best garden he achieved,And of it left his son imperial lord.Henry the Sixth, in infant bands crown'd KingOf France and England, did this king succeed;Whose state so many had the managing,That they lost France and made his England bleed:Which oft our stage hath shown; and, for their sake,In your fair minds let this acceptance take.

Trumpet sounds.

May God, the best marriage maker, combine your hearts as one and your realms! As man and wife are one in love, may also your kingdoms, so they may never have discord again. May English and French receive each other in good will. Amen!

Amen!

Let's prepare for our wedding. On that day, I'll take your oath of loyalty, my Lord Burgundy and all my peers. I will swear to Kate and you to me, and may they uphold and prosper.

Exit.

Enter Chorus.

Thus, we end our attempt at telling this story of mighty men in such a little room. Unfortunately, we could not bring them their due glory. In the short time in which he lived, our hero was a great warrior and created the world's greatest garden, France, leaving his son, Henry the Sixth, as ruler. While many had their hands in his affairs, France was lost and England at civil war, which has been portrayed on this stage before. So, please accept this play with your fair minds.

Made in the USA
Lexington, KY
02 December 2015